MznLnx

Missing Links Exam Preps

Exam Prep for

Cost Management: Stratagies for Business Decisions

Hilton, Maher & Selto, 3rd Edition

The MznLnx Exam Prep is your link from the texbook and lecture to your exams.
The MznLnx Exam Preps are unauthorized and comprehensive reviews of your textbooks.

All material provided by MznLnx and Rico Publications (c) 2010
Textbook publishers and textbook authors do not particpate in or contribute to these reviews.

MznLnx

Rico Publications

Exam Prep for Cost Management: Stratagies for Business Decisions
3rd Edition
Hilton, Maher & Selto

Publisher: Raymond Houge
Assistant Editor: Michael Rouger
Text and Cover Designer: Lisa Buckner
Marketing Manager: Sara Swagger
Project Manager, Editorial Production: Jerry Emerson
Art Director: Vernon Lowerui

Product Manager: Dave Mason
Editorial Assitant: Rachel Guzmanji
Pedagogy: Debra Long
Cover Image: Jim Reed/Getty Images
Text and Cover Printer: City Printing, Inc.
Compositor: Media Mix, Inc.

(c) 2010 Rico Publications

ALL RIGHTS RESERVED. No part of this work covered by the copyright may be reproduced or used in any form or by an means--graphic, electronic, or mechanical, including photocopying, recording, taping, Web distribution, information storage, and retrieval systems, or in any other manner--without the written permission of the publisher.

For more information about our products, contact us at:
Dave.Mason@RicoPublications.com

For permission to use material from this text or product, submit a request online to:
Dave.Mason@RicoPublications.com

Printed in the United States
ISBN:

Contents

CHAPTER 1
Cost Management and Strategic Decision Making — 1

CHAPTER 2
Product Costing Systems: Concepts and Design Issues — 8

CHAPTER 3
Cost Accumulation for Job-Shop and Batch Production Operations — 16

CHAPTER 4
Activity-Based Costing Systems — 23

CHAPTER 5
Activity-Based Management — 26

CHAPTER 6
Managing Customer Profitability — 30

CHAPTER 7
Managing Quality and Time to Create Value — 36

CHAPTER 8
Process-Costing Systems — 46

CHAPTER 9
Joint-Process Costing — 49

CHAPTER 10
Managing and Allocating Support-Service Costs — 53

CHAPTER 11
Cost Estimation — 57

CHAPTER 12
Financial and CostVolume-Profit Models — 63

CHAPTER 13
Cost Management and Decision Making — 68

CHAPTER 14
Strategic Issues in Making Investment Decisions — 73

CHAPTER 15
Budgeting and Financial Planning — 81

CHAPTER 16
Standard Costing, Variance Analysis, and Kaizen Costing — 88

CHAPTER 17
Flexible Budgets, Overhead Cost Management, and Activity-Based Budgeting — 94

CHAPTER 18
Organizational Design, Responsibility Accounting, and Evaluation — 98

CHAPTER 19
Transfer Pricing — 103

CHAPTER 20
Strategy, Balanced Scorecards, and Incentive Systems — 107

ANSWER KEY — 116

TO THE STUDENT

COMPREHENSIVE

The *MznLnx* Exam Prep series is designed to help you pass your exams. Editors at MznLnx review your textbooks and then prepare these practice exams to help you master the textbook material. Unlike study guides, workbooks, and practice tests provided by the texbook publisher and textbook authors, *MznLnx* gives you **all** of the material in each chapter in exam form, not just samples, so you can be sure to nail your exam.

MECHANICAL

The MznLnx Exam Prep series creates exams that will help you learn the subject matter as well as test you on your understanding. Each question is designed to help you master the concept. Just working through the exams, you gain an understanding of the subject--its a simple mechanical process that produces success.

INTEGRATED STUDY GUIDE AND REVIEW

MznLnx is not just a set of exams designed to test you, its also a comprehensive review of the subject content. Each exam question is also a review of the concept, making sure that you will get the answer correct without having to go to other sources of material. You learn as you go! Its the easiest way to pass an exam.

HUMOR

Studying can be tedious and dry. MznLnx's instructional design includes moderate humor within the exam questions on occassion, to break the tedium and revitalize the brain

Chapter 1. Cost Management and Strategic Decision Making 1

1. An _____ is a practitioner of accountancy, which is the measurement, disclosure or provision of assurance about financial information that helps managers, investors, tax authorities and other decision makers make resource allocation decisions.

The word '_____' is derived from the French 'Compter' which took its origin from the Latin 'Computare'. The word was formerly written in English as 'Accomptant', but in process of time the word, which was always pronounced by dropping the 'p', became gradually changed both in pronunciation and in orthography to its present form.

   a. A Stake in the Outcome
   b. A4e
   c. AAAI
   d. Accountant

2. The _____ of a company or public agency is the corporate officer primarily responsible for managing the financial risks of the business or agency. This officer is also responsible for financial planning and record-keeping, as well as financial reporting to higher management. (In recent years, however, the role has expanded to encompass communicating financial performance and forecasts to the analyst community.)
   a. 28-hour day
   b. 1990 Clean Air Act
   c. 33 Strategies of War
   d. Chief financial officer

3. A _____ is a professional who provides advice in a particular area of expertise such as management, accountancy, the environment, entertainment, technology, law , human resources, marketing, medicine, finance, economics, public affairs, communication, engineering, sound system design, graphic design, or waste management.

A _____ is usually an expert or a professional in a specific field and has a wide knowledge of the subject matter. A _____ usually works for a consultancy firm or is self-employed, and engages with multiple and changing clients.

   a. 28-hour day
   b. 33 Strategies of War
   c. 1990 Clean Air Act
   d. Consultant

4. In economics, business, retail, and accounting, a _____ is the value of money that has been used up to produce something, and hence is not available for use anymore. In economics, a _____ is an alternative that is given up as a result of a decision. In business, the _____ may be one of acquisition, in which case the amount of money expended to acquire it is counted as _____.
   a. Cost allocation
   b. Fixed costs
   c. Cost overrun
   d. Cost

5. A _____, securities analyst, research analyst, equity analyst, or investment analyst is a person who performs financial analysis for external or internal clients as a core part of the job.

An analyst studies companies and other entities to arrive at the estimate of their financial value. It is normally done by analyzing financial reports, aided by follow-up interviews with company representatives and industry experts.

   a. Financial analyst
   b. Portfolio manager
   c. Purchasing manager
   d. Director of communications

Chapter 1. Cost Management and Strategic Decision Making

6. _____ is a term defined by the Oxford English Dictionary as an individual's 'course or progress through life '. It is usually considered to pertain to remunerative work (and sometimes also formal education.)

The etymology of the term is somewhat ironic in that it comes from the Latin word carrera, which means race .

    a. Nursing shortage
    c. Career planning
    b. Spatial mismatch
    d. Career

7. _____ is the difference between the revenues earned from and the costs associated with the customer relationship in a specified period.

According to Philip Kotler,'a profitable customer is a person, household or a company that overtime, yields a revenue stream that exceeds by an acceptable amount the company's cost stream of attracting, selling and servicing the customer'

Although _____ is nothing more than the result of applying the business concept of profit to a customer relationship, measuring the profitability of a firm's customers or customer groups can often deliver useful business insights.

Quite often a very small percentage of the firm's best customers will account for a large portion of firm profit.

    a. Process costing
    c. Customer profitability
    b. Factory overhead
    d. Profit center

8. _____ is, in very basic words, a position a firm occupies against its competitors.

According to Michael Porter, the three methods for creating a sustainable _____ are through:

1. Cost leadership

2. Differentiation

3. Focus (economics)

    a. 28-hour day
    c. 1990 Clean Air Act
    b. Competitive advantage
    d. Theory Z

9. _____ can be regarded as an outcome of mental processes (cognitive process) leading to the selection of a course of action among several alternatives. Every _____ process produces a final choice. The output can be an action or an opinion of choice.

    a. Decision making
    c. 33 Strategies of War
    b. 1990 Clean Air Act
    d. 28-hour day

10. In decision theory and estimation theory, the _____ of an estimator, $\hat{\theta}$, of an unknown parameter of the distribution, θ, is the expected value of the loss function

$$R(\theta, \hat{\theta}) = \mathbb{E}_\theta L(\theta, \hat{\theta}) = \int L(\theta, \hat{\theta})\, dP_\theta.$$

where dP_θ is a probability measure parametrized by θ.

- For a scalar parameter θ and a quadratic loss function,

$$L(\theta, \hat{\theta}) = (\theta - \hat{\theta})^2$$

the _____ function becomes the mean squared error of the estimate,

$$R(\theta, \hat{\theta}) = E_\theta (\theta - \hat{\theta})^2$$

- In density estimation, the unknown parameter is probability density itself. The loss function is typically chosen to be a norm in an appropriate function space. For example, for L^2 norm,

$$L(f, \hat{f}) = \|f - \hat{f}\|_2^2$$

the _____ function becomes the mean integrated squared error

$$R(f, \hat{f}) = E\|f - \hat{f}\|^2$$

a. Financial modeling
b. Risk
c. Linear model
d. Risk aversion

11. In business, a _____ is a product or a business unit that generates unusually high profit margins: so high that it is responsible for a large amount of a company's operating profit. This profit far exceeds the amount necessary to maintain the _____ business, and the excess is used by the business for other purposes.

A firm is said to be acting as a _____ when its earnings per share (EPS) is equal to its dividends per share (DPS), or in other words, when a firm pays out 100% of its free cash flow (FCF) to its shareholders as dividends at the end of each accounting term.

a. Workflow
b. Cash cow
c. Middle management
d. Design management in organization

12. The phrase _____, according to the Organization for Economic Co-operation and Development, refers to 'creative work undertaken on a systematic basis in order to increase the stock of knowledge, including knowledge of man, culture and society, and the use of this stock of knowledge to devise new applications [sic]'

New product design and development is more than often a crucial factor in the survival of a company. In an industry that is fast changing, firms must continually revise their design and range of products. This is necessary due to continuous technology change and development as well as other competitors and the changing preference of customers.

a. 33 Strategies of War
c. 28-hour day
b. Research and development
d. 1990 Clean Air Act

13. The _____ is a concept from business management that was first described and popularized by Michael Porter in his 1985 best-seller, Competitive Advantage: Creating and Sustaining Superior Performance.

A _____ is a chain of activities. Products pass through all activities of the chain in order and at each activity the product gains some value. The chain of activities gives the products more added value than the sum of added values of all activities. It is important not to mix the concept of the _____ with the costs occurring throughout the activities.

a. Market development
c. Mass marketing
b. Customer relationship management
d. Value chain

14. _____ is the provision of service to customers before, during and after a purchase.

According to Turban et al. (2002), '_____ is a series of activities designed to enhance the level of customer satisfaction - that is, the feeling that a product or service has met the customer expectation.'

Its importance varies by product, industry and customer; defective or broken merchandise can be exchanged, often only with a receipt and within a specified time frame.

a. Service rate
c. 28-hour day
b. Customer service
d. 1990 Clean Air Act

15. _____ is one of the four elements of marketing mix. An organization or set of organizations (go-betweens) involved in the process of making a product or service available for use or consumption by a consumer or business user.

The other three parts of the marketing mix are product, pricing, and promotion.

a. Matching theory
c. Missing completely at random
b. Job creation programs
d. Distribution

16. _____ is an integrated communications-based process through which individuals and communities discover that existing and newly-identified needs and wants may be satisfied by the products and services of others.

Chapter 1. Cost Management and Strategic Decision Making 5

_____ is defined by the American _____ Association as the activity, set of institutions, and processes for creating, communicating, delivering, and exchanging offerings that have value for customers, clients, partners, and society at large. The term developed from the original meaning which referred literally to going to market, as in shopping, or going to a market to buy or sell goods or services.

- a. Market development
- b. Customer relationship management
- c. Disruptive technology
- d. Marketing

17. _____ is subcontracting a process, such as product design or manufacturing, to a third-party company. The decision to outsource is often made in the interest of lowering cost or making better use of time and energy costs, redirecting or conserving energy directed at the competencies of a particular business, or to make more efficient use of land, labor, capital, (information) technology and resources. _____ became part of the business lexicon during the 1980s.
- a. Opinion leadership
- b. Operant conditioning
- c. Unemployment insurance
- d. Outsourcing

18. In marketing, _____ is the process of distinguishing the differences of a product or offering from others, to make it more attractive to a particular target market. This involves differentiating it from competitors' products as well as one's own product offerings.
- a. Product differentiation
- b. PEST analysis
- c. Market development
- d. Market share

19. _____ is an advertisement in which a particular product specifically mentions a competitor by name for the express purpose of showing why the competitor is inferior to the product naming it.

This should not be confused with parody advertisements, where a fictional product is being advertised for the purpose of poking fun at the particular advertisement, nor should it be confused with the use of a coined brand name for the purpose of comparing the product without actually naming an actual competitor. ('Wikipedia tastes better and is less filling than the Encyclopedia Galactica.')

In the 1980s, during what has been referred to as the cola wars, soft-drink manufacturer Pepsi ran a series of advertisements where people, caught on hidden camera, in a blind taste test, chose Pepsi over rival Coca-Cola.

- a. 33 Strategies of War
- b. Comparative advertising
- c. 1990 Clean Air Act
- d. 28-hour day

20. _____ is a structured approach to transitioning individuals, teams, and organizations from a current state to a desired future state. The current definition of _____ includes both organizational _____ processes and individual _____ models, which together are used to manage the people side of change.

A number of models are available for understanding the transitioning of individuals through the phases of _____ and strengthening organizational development initiative in both government and corporate sectors.

a. 1990 Clean Air Act
c. 28-hour day
b. 33 Strategies of War
d. Change management

21. _____ has been described as the 'process of social influence in which one person can enlist the aid and support of others in the accomplishment of a common task'. A definition more inclusive of followers comes from Alan Keith of Genentech who said '_____ is ultimately about creating a way for people to contribute to making something extraordinary happen.'

_____ is one of the most salient aspects of the organizational context. However, defining _____ has been challenging.

a. 28-hour day
c. 1990 Clean Air Act
b. Situational leadership
d. Leadership

22. A _____ is a group of employees from various functional areas of the organization - research, engineering, marketing, finance. human resources, and operations, for example - who are all focused on a specific objective and are responsible to work as a team to improve coordination and innovation across divisions and resolve mutual problems.

a. Sociotechnical systems
c. Cross-functional team
b. Goal-setting theory
d. Graduate recruitment

23. _____ refers to the movement of cash into or out of a business or financial product. It is usually measured during a specified, finite period of time. Measurement of _____ can be used

- to determine a project's rate of return or value. The time of _____s into and out of projects are used as inputs in financial models such as internal rate of return, and net present value.
- to determine problems with a business's liquidity. Being profitable does not necessarily mean being liquid. A company can fail because of a shortage of cash, even while profitable.
- as an alternate measure of a business's profits when it is believed that accrual accounting concepts do not represent economic realities. For example, a company may be notionally profitable but generating little operational cash (as may be the case for a company that barters its products rather than selling for cash.) In such a case, the company may be deriving additional operating cash by issuing shares evaluating default risk, re-investment requirements, etc.

_____ is a generic term used differently depending on the context. It may be defined by users for their own purposes.

a. Cash flow
c. Gross profit
b. Sweat equity
d. Gross profit margin

24. _____ was a writer, management consultant, and self-described 'social ecologist.' Widely considered to be 'the father of modern management,' his 39 books and countless scholarly and popular articles explored how humans are organized across all sectors of society--in business, government and the nonprofit world. His writings have predicted many of the major developments of the late twentieth century, including privatization and decentralization; the rise of Japan to economic world power; the decisive importance of marketing; and the emergence of the information society with its necessity of lifelong learning. In 1959, Drucker coined the term 'knowledge worker' and later in his life considered knowledge work productivity to be the next frontier of management.

a. Peter Ferdinand Drucker
b. Debora L. Spar
c. Jacques Al-Salawat Nasruddin Nasser
d. Chrissie Hynde

25. _____, in marketing, manufacturing, call centres and management, is the use of flexible computer-aided manufacturing systems to produce custom output. Those systems combine the low unit costs of mass production processes with the flexibility of individual customization.

'_____' is the new frontier in business competition for both manufacturing and service industries.

a. 33 Strategies of War
b. 1990 Clean Air Act
c. 28-hour day
d. Mass customization

26. _____ is a civil designation for persons who are incorporated in a fixed or permanent way to a society or group: regular member of the working staff, permanent staff distinguished from a supernumerary.

The term '_____' and its counterpart, 'supernumerary,' originated in Spanish and Latin American academy and government; it is now also used in countries all over the world, such as France, the U.S., England, Italy, etc.

There are _____ members of surgical organizations, of universities, of gastronomical associations, etc.

a. Affiliation
b. Adam Smith
c. Abraham Harold Maslow
d. Numerary

27. In game theory, an _____ is a set of moves or strategies taken by the players, or their payoffs resulting from the actions or strategies taken by all players. The two are complementary in that given knowledge of the set of strategies of all players, the final state of the game is known, as are any relevant payoffs. In a game where chance or a random event is involved, the _____ is not known from only the set of strategies, but is only realized when the random event(s) are realized.

a. A Stake in the Outcome
b. A4e
c. AAAI
d. Outcome

28. In operant conditioning, _____ occurs when an event following a response causes an increase in the probability of that response occurring in the future. Response strength can be assessed by measures such as the frequency with which the response is made (for example, a pigeon may peck a key more times in the session), or the speed with which it is made (for example, a rat may run a maze faster.) The environment change contingent upon the response is called a reinforcer.

a. Meetings, Incentives, Conferences, and Exhibitions
b. Historiometry
c. Diminishing Manufacturing Sources and Material Shortages
d. Reinforcement

Chapter 2. Product Costing Systems: Concepts and Design Issues

1. In economics, business, retail, and accounting, a _____ is the value of money that has been used up to produce something, and hence is not available for use anymore. In economics, a _____ is an alternative that is given up as a result of a decision. In business, the _____ may be one of acquisition, in which case the amount of money expended to acquire it is counted as _____.

   a. Cost overrun
   b. Cost allocation
   c. Fixed costs
   d. Cost

2. _____ is, in very basic words, a position a firm occupies against its competitors.

   According to Michael Porter, the three methods for creating a sustainable _____ are through:

   1. Cost leadership

   2. Differentiation

   3. Focus (economics)

   a. 1990 Clean Air Act
   b. 28-hour day
   c. Theory Z
   d. Competitive advantage

3. _____ is the process whereby companies use cost accounting to report or control the various costs of doing business.

   _____ generally describes the approaches and activities of managers in short run and long run planning and control decisions that increase value for customers and lower costs of products and services.

   a. Strict liability
   b. Genbutsu
   c. Missing completely at random
   d. Cost management

4. _____ is a company's financial statement that indicates how the revenue is transformed into the net income The purpose of the _____ is to show managers and investors whether the company made or lost money during the period being reported.

   The important thing to remember about an _____ is that it represents a period of time.

   a. A4e
   b. AAAI
   c. A Stake in the Outcome
   d. Income statement

5. _____ in manufacturing refers to processes that occur later on in a production sequence or production line.

   Viewing a company 'from order to cash' might have high-level processes such as Marketing, Sales, Order Entry, Manufacturing, Packaging, Shipping, Invoicing. Each of these could be deconstructed into many sub-processes and supporting processes.

Chapter 2. Product Costing Systems: Concepts and Design Issues

a. Downstream
c. Genbutsu
b. Science Learning Centre
d. Probability-generating function

6. The _____ is a concept from business management that was first described and popularized by Michael Porter in his 1985 best-seller, Competitive Advantage: Creating and Sustaining Superior Performance.

A _____ is a chain of activities. Products pass through all activities of the chain in order and at each activity the product gains some value. The chain of activities gives the products more added value than the sum of added values of all activities. It is important not to mix the concept of the _____ with the costs occurring throughout the activities.

a. Mass marketing
c. Market development
b. Customer relationship management
d. Value chain

7. In financial accounting, _____ or cost of sales includes the direct costs attributable to the production of the goods sold by a company. This amount includes the materials cost used in creating the goods along with the direct labour costs used to produce the good. It excludes indirect expenses such as distribution costs and sales force costs.

a. Reorder point
c. 28-hour day
b. 1990 Clean Air Act
d. Cost of goods sold

8. _____ are formal records of the financial activities of a business, person, or other entity. In British English, including United Kingdom company law, _____ are often referred to as accounts, although the term _____ is also used, particularly by accountants.

_____ provide an overview of a business or person's financial condition in both short and long term.

a. 1990 Clean Air Act
c. 33 Strategies of War
b. 28-hour day
d. Financial statements

9. _____ is an advertisement in which a particular product specifically mentions a competitor by name for the express purpose of showing why the competitor is inferior to the product naming it.

This should not be confused with parody advertisements, where a fictional product is being advertised for the purpose of poking fun at the particular advertisement, nor should it be confused with the use of a coined brand name for the purpose of comparing the product without actually naming an actual competitor. ('Wikipedia tastes better and is less filling than the Encyclopedia Galactica.')

In the 1980s, during what has been referred to as the cola wars, soft-drink manufacturer Pepsi ran a series of advertisements where people, caught on hidden camera, in a blind taste test, chose Pepsi over rival Coca-Cola.

a. 33 Strategies of War
c. 1990 Clean Air Act
b. 28-hour day
d. Comparative advertising

10. _____ is a costing model that identifies activities in an organization and assigns the cost of each activity resource to all products and services according to the actual consumption by each: it assigns more indirect costs (overhead) into direct costs.

In this way an organization can establish the true cost of its individual products and services for the purposes of identifying and eliminating those which are unprofitable and lowering the prices of those which are overpriced.

In a business organization, the ABC methodology assigns an organization's resource costs through activities to the products and services provided to its customers.

a. A4e
b. A Stake in the Outcome
c. Indirect costs
d. Activity-based costing

11. A _____ is a process in which a potential employee is evaluated by an employer for prospective employment in their company, organization and was established in the late 16th century.

A _____ typically precedes the hiring decision, and is used to evaluate the candidate. The interview is usually preceded by the evaluation of submitted résumés from interested candidates, then selecting a small number of candidates for interviews.

a. Supported employment
b. Job interview
c. Payrolling
d. Split shift

12. _____, Gross profit margin or Gross Profit Rate can be defined as the amount of contribution to the business enterprise, after paying for direct-fixed and direct-variable unit costs, required to cover overheads (fixed commitments) and provide a buffer for unknown items. It expresses the relationship between gross profit and sales revenue.

It can be expressed in absolute terms:

Gross Profit = Revenue − Cost of Sales

or as the ratio of gross profit to sales revenue, usually in the form of a percentage:

_____ Percentage = (Revenue-Cost of Sales)/Revenue

Cost of Sales includes variable costs and fixed costs directly linked to the product, such as material and labor.

a. Profit maximization
b. Gross margin
c. 1990 Clean Air Act
d. Profit margin

13. _____ is an integrated communications-based process through which individuals and communities discover that existing and newly-identified needs and wants may be satisfied by the products and services of others.

_____ is defined by the American _____ Association as the activity, set of institutions, and processes for creating, communicating, delivering, and exchanging offerings that have value for customers, clients, partners, and society at large. The term developed from the original meaning which referred literally to going to market, as in shopping, or going to a market to buy or sell goods or services.

Chapter 2. Product Costing Systems: Concepts and Design Issues   11

   a. Marketing
   c. Market development
   b. Customer relationship management
   d. Disruptive technology

   14. _____ is a measure of a company's earning power from ongoing operations, equal to earnings before the deduction of interest payments and income taxes.

To accountants, economic profit, or EP, is a single-period metric to determine the value created by a company in one period - usually a year. It is the net profit after tax less the equity charge, a risk-weighted cost of capital.

   a. A4e
   c. A Stake in the Outcome
   b. AAAI
   d. Operating profit

   15. _____ is a term used in accounting, economics and finance to spread the cost of an asset over the span of several years.

In simple words we can say that _____ is the reduction in the value of an asset due to usage, passage of time, wear and tear, technological outdating or obsolescence, depletion, inadequacy, rot, rust, decay or other such factors.

In accounting, _____ is a term used to describe any method of attributing the historical or purchase cost of an asset across its useful life, roughly corresponding to normal wear and tear.

   a. Treasury stock
   c. Matching principle
   b. Net profit
   d. Depreciation

   16. _____ is the total cost involved in operating all production facilities of a manufacturing business. It generally applies to indirect labor and indirect cost, it also includes all costs involved in manufacturing with the exception of the cost of raw materials and direct labor. _____ also includes certain costs such as quality assurance costs, cleanup costs, and property insurance premiums.
   a. Customer profitability
   c. Process costing
   b. Factory overhead
   d. Profit center

   17. _____ is the amount of time someone works beyond normal working hours. Normal hours may be determined in several ways:

   - by custom (what is considered healthy or reasonable by society),
   - by practices of a given trade or profession,
   - by legislation,
   - by agreement between employers and workers or their representatives.

Most nations have _____ laws designed to dissuade or prevent employers from forcing their employees to work excessively long hours. These laws may take into account other considerations than the humanitarian, such as increasing the overall level of employment in the economy. One common approach to regulating _____ is to require employers to pay workers at a higher hourly rate for _____ work.

Chapter 2. Product Costing Systems: Concepts and Design Issues

a. Industrial relations
b. Organizational effectiveness
c. Organizational structure
d. Overtime

18. _____ are goods that have completed the manufacturing process but have not yet been sold or distributed to the end user.

Manufacturing has three classes of inventory:

1. Raw material
2. Work in process
3. _____

A good purchased as a 'raw material' goes into the manufacture of a product. A good only partially completed during the manufacturing process is called 'work in process'. When the good is completed as to manufacturing but not yet sold or distributed to the end-user is called a 'finished good'.

a. 28-hour day
b. Reorder point
c. 1990 Clean Air Act
d. Finished goods

19. _____ is an inventory strategy that strives to improve the return on investment of a business by reducing in-process inventory and its associated carrying costs. To meet _____ objectives, the process relies on signals between different points in the process. This means the process is often driven by a series of signals, or Kanban, which tell production when to make the next part. Kanban are usually 'tickets' but can be simple visual signals, such as the presence or absence of a part on a shelf. Implemented correctly, _____ can dramatically improve a manufacturing organization's return on investment, quality, and efficiency.

a. 28-hour day
b. 1990 Clean Air Act
c. 33 Strategies of War
d. Just-in-time

20. In economics, the _____ is the theory that the price of an object or condition is determined by the sum of the cost of the resources that went into making it. The cost can compose any of the factors of production (including labour, capital, or land) and taxation.

The theory makes the most sense under assumptions of constant returns to scale and the existence of just one non-produced factor of production.

a. 33 Strategies of War
b. 1990 Clean Air Act
c. Cost-of-production theory of value
d. 28-hour day

21. In economics, _____ are business expenses that are not dependent on the activities of the business They tend to be time-related, such as salaries or rents being paid per month. This is in contrast to variable costs, which are volume-related (and are paid per quantity.)

In management accounting, _____ are defined as expenses that do not change in proportion to the activity of a business, within the relevant period or scale of production.

Chapter 2. Product Costing Systems: Concepts and Design Issues

a. Cost of quality
b. Fixed costs
c. Transaction cost
d. Cost allocation

22. _____s are expenses that change in proportion to the activity of a business. In other words, _____ is the sum of marginal costs. It can also be considered normal costs.
   a. Fixed costs
   b. Cost accounting
   c. Cost overrun
   d. Variable cost

23. The _____ of a product is the cost per standard unit supplied, which may be a single sample or a container of a given number. When purchasing more than a single unit, the total cost will increase with the number of units, but it is common for the _____ to decrease as quantity is increased (bulk purchasing), as there are discounts etc. This reduction in long run _____s which arise from an increase in production/purchasing is due to the fixed costs being spread out over more products and is called economies of scale.
   a. A Stake in the Outcome
   b. A4e
   c. AAAI
   d. Unit cost

24. _____ is a term used to define maximum possible output of an economy. According to UNCTAD, no agreed-upon definition exists. UNCTAD itself proposes: 'the productive resources, entrepreneurial capabilities and production linkages which together determine the capacity of a country to produce goods and services.' The term '_____' is also used in binary economics to mean income-generating capacity be it of a factory, land, patent or the labour skills of an individual.
   a. Diseconomies of scale
   b. Factors of production
   c. Productive capacity
   d. Multifactor productivity

25. _____ or economic opportunity loss is the value of the next best alternative forgone as the result of making a decision. _____ analysis is an important part of a company's decision-making processes but is not treated as an actual cost in any financial statement. The next best thing that a person can engage in is referred to as the _____ of doing the best thing and ignoring the next best thing to be done.
   a. AAAI
   b. Opportunity cost
   c. A Stake in the Outcome
   d. A4e

26. In economics and business decision-making, _____ are costs that cannot be recovered once they have been incurred. _____ are sometimes contrasted with variable costs, which are the costs that will change due to the proposed course of action, and prospective costs which are costs that will be incurred if an action is taken.

In traditional microeconomic theory, only variable costs are relevant to a decision.

   a. Pygmalion effect
   b. Sunk costs
   c. Cognitive biases
   d. Fundamental attribution error

27. _____ can be regarded as an outcome of mental processes (cognitive process) leading to the selection of a course of action among several alternatives. Every _____ process produces a final choice. The output can be an action or an opinion of choice.
   a. Decision making
   b. 33 Strategies of War
   c. 28-hour day
   d. 1990 Clean Air Act

Chapter 2. Product Costing Systems: Concepts and Design Issues

28. _____ are costs that are not directly accountable to a particular function or product. _____ may be either fixed or variable. _____ include taxes, administration, personnel and security costs, and are also known as overhead.
   a. A4e
   b. A Stake in the Outcome
   c. Activity-based management
   d. Indirect costs

29. In logistics, _____ refers to the capability for tracing goods along the distribution chain on a batch number or series number basis. _____ is an important aspect for example in the automotive industry, where it makes recalls possible, or in the food industry where it contributes to food safety.

   The international standards organization EPCglobal under GS1 has ratified the EPCglobal Network standards which codify the syntax and semantics for supply chain events and the secure method for selectively sharing supply chain events with trading partners. Theses standards for _____ have been used in successful deployments in many industries and there are now a wide range of products that are certified as being compatible with these standards.

   a. 28-hour day
   b. 1990 Clean Air Act
   c. Traceability
   d. 33 Strategies of War

30. _____ is a process of attributing cost to particular cost centres. For example the wage of the driver of the purchasing department can be allocated to the purchasing department cost centre. It is not necessary to share the wage cost over several different cost centers.cost and services are not identical to each other.
   a. Cost allocation
   b. Fixed costs
   c. Cost accounting
   d. Cost overrun

31. The _____ is the labour pool in employment. It is generally used to describe those working for a single company or industry, but can also apply to a geographic region like a city, country, state, etc. The term generally excludes the employers or management, and implies those involved in manual labour.
   a. Division of labour
   b. Workforce
   c. Work-life balance
   d. Pink-collar worker

32. Total _____ is a method of Accounting cost which entails the full cost of manufacturing or providing a service. This includes not just the costs of materials and labour, but also of all manufacturing overheads (whether 'fixed' or 'variable'.) One of the main reasons for absorbing overheads into the cost of units is for inventory valuation purposes.
   a. AAAI
   b. A Stake in the Outcome
   c. Absorption costing
   d. A4e

33. _____ is the difference between operating revenues and operating expenses, but it is also sometimes used as a synonym for EBIT and operating profit. This is true if the firm has no non-_____.

   A professional investor contemplating a change to the capital structure of a firm first evaluates a firm's fundamental earnings potential (reflected by Earnings Before Interest, Taxes, Depreciation and Amortization EBITDA and EBIT), and then determines the optimal use of debt vs. equity.

   a. A Stake in the Outcome
   b. AAAI
   c. A4e
   d. Operating income

Chapter 2. Product Costing Systems: Concepts and Design Issues

34. In cost-volume-profit analysis, a form of management accounting, _____ is the marginal profit per unit sale. It is a useful quantity in carrying out various calculations, and can be used as a measure of operating leverage.

The Total _____ is Total Revenue (TR, or Sales) minus Total Variable Cost (TVC):

TContribution margin = TR − TVC

The Unit _____ (C) is Unit Revenue (Price, P) minus Unit Variable Cost (V):

C = P − V

The _____ Ratio is the percentage of Contribution over Total Revenue, which can be calculated from the unit contribution over unit price or total contribution over Total Revenue:

$$\frac{C}{P} = \frac{P-V}{P} = \frac{\text{Unit Contribution Margin}}{\text{Price}} = \frac{\text{Total Contribution Margin}}{\text{Total Revenue}}$$

For instance, if the price is $10 and the unit variable cost is $2, then the unit _____ is $8, and the _____ ratio is $8/$10 = 80%.

a. Customer profitability
c. Factory overhead
b. Contribution margin
d. Profit center

35. _____ is one of the four Ps of the marketing mix. The other three aspects are product, promotion, and place. It is also a key variable in microeconomic price allocation theory.
a. Pricing
c. Price floor
b. Transfer pricing
d. Penetration pricing

36. In business and accounting, _____s are everything of value that is owned by a person or company. Any property or object of value that one possesses, usually considered as applicable to the payment of one's debts is considered an _____. Simplistically stated, _____s are things of value that can be readily converted into cash.
a. Asset
c. AAAI
b. A Stake in the Outcome
d. A4e

Chapter 3. Cost Accumulation for Job-Shop and Batch Production Operations

1. _____ is an accounting methodology that traces and accumulates direct costs, and allocates indirect costs of a manufacturing process. Costs are assigned to products, usually in a large batch, which might include an entire month's production. Eventually, costs have to be allocated to individual units of product.
   a. Customer profitability
   b. Factory overhead
   c. Process costing
   d. Profit center

2. _____ refers to the movement of cash into or out of a business or financial product. It is usually measured during a specified, finite period of time. Measurement of _____ can be used

   - to determine a project's rate of return or value. The time of _____s into and out of projects are used as inputs in financial models such as internal rate of return, and net present value.
   - to determine problems with a business's liquidity. Being profitable does not necessarily mean being liquid. A company can fail because of a shortage of cash, even while profitable.
   - as an alternate measure of a business's profits when it is believed that accrual accounting concepts do not represent economic realities. For example, a company may be notionally profitable but generating little operational cash (as may be the case for a company that barters its products rather than selling for cash.) In such a case, the company may be deriving additional operating cash by issuing shares evaluating default risk, re-investment requirements, etc.

   _____ is a generic term used differently depending on the context. It may be defined by users for their own purposes.

   a. Gross profit
   b. Cash flow
   c. Sweat equity
   d. Gross profit margin

3. _____ is the discipline of planning, organizing and managing resources to bring about the successful completion of specific project goals and objectives. It is often closely related to and sometimes conflated with Program management.

   A project is a finite endeavor--having specific start and completion dates--undertaken to meet particular goals and objectives, usually to bring about beneficial change or added value.

   a. Precedence diagram
   b. Project engineer
   c. Work package
   d. Project management

4. _____ consists of the mental process of thinking involved with the process of judging the merits of multiple options and selecting one of them for action. Some simple examples include deciding whether to get up in the morning or go back to sleep, or selecting a given route for a journey. More complex examples (often decisions that affect what a person thinks or their core beliefs) include choosing a lifestyle, religious affiliation, or political position.
   a. Groups decision making
   b. Championship mobilization
   c. Trade study
   d. Choice

5. _____ is a company's financial statement that indicates how the revenue is transformed into the net income The purpose of the _____ is to show managers and investors whether the company made or lost money during the period being reported.

   The important thing to remember about an _____ is that it represents a period of time.

a. A Stake in the Outcome
b. A4e
c. AAAI
d. Income statement

6. In economics, business, retail, and accounting, a _____ is the value of money that has been used up to produce something, and hence is not available for use anymore. In economics, a _____ is an alternative that is given up as a result of a decision. In business, the _____ may be one of acquisition, in which case the amount of money expended to acquire it is counted as _____.
a. Cost allocation
b. Cost
c. Fixed costs
d. Cost overrun

7. The _____ is a concept from business management that was first described and popularized by Michael Porter in his 1985 best-seller, Competitive Advantage: Creating and Sustaining Superior Performance.

A _____ is a chain of activities. Products pass through all activities of the chain in order and at each activity the product gains some value. The chain of activities gives the products more added value than the sum of added values of all activities. It is important not to mix the concept of the _____ with the costs occurring throughout the activities.

a. Market development
b. Mass marketing
c. Customer relationship management
d. Value chain

8. In probability theory, a probability distribution is called _____ if its cumulative distribution function is _____. This is equivalent to saying that for random variables X with the distribution in question, Pr[X = a] = 0 for all real numbers a, i.e.: the probability that X attains the value a is zero, for any number a. If the distribution of X is _____ then X is called a _____ random variable.
a. Decision tree pruning
b. Connectionist expert systems
c. Pay Band
d. Continuous

9. _____ is one of the managerial functions like planning, organizing, staffing and directing. It is an important function because it helps to check the errors and to take the corrective action so that deviation from standards are minimized and stated goals of the organization are achieved in desired manner. According to modern concepts, _____ is a foreseeing action whereas earlier concept of _____ was used only when errors were detected. _____ in management means setting standards, measuring actual performance and taking corrective action.
a. Turnover
b. Schedule of reinforcement
c. Control
d. Decision tree pruning

10. The _____ of an edge is $c_f(u,v) = c(u,v) - f(u,v)$. This defines a residual network denoted $G_f(V, E_f)$, giving the amount of available capacity. See that there can be an edge from u to v in the residual network, even though there is no edge from u to v in the original network.
a. 1990 Clean Air Act
b. 28-hour day
c. 33 Strategies of War
d. Residual capacity

Chapter 3. Cost Accumulation for Job-Shop and Batch Production Operations

11. Total _____ is a method of Accounting cost which entails the full cost of manufacturing or providing a service. This includes not just the costs of materials and labour, but also of all manufacturing overheads (whether 'fixed' or 'variable'.) One of the main reasons for absorbing overheads into the cost of units is for inventory valuation purposes.
    a. A Stake in the Outcome
    b. AAAI
    c. Absorption costing
    d. A4e

12. A _____ is the rate used to apply manufacturing overhead to work-in-process inventory. It is calculated as estimated manufacturing overhead cost divided by estimated amount of cost driver or activity base. Common activity bases used in the calculation include direct labor costs, direct labor hours, or machine hours.
    a. Safety stock
    b. Business ecosystem
    c. Pre-determined overhead rate
    d. Planning horizon

13. A _____, in business matters, is an entity that is controlled by a bigger and more powerful entity. The controlled entity is called a company, corporation, or limited liability company and in some cases can be a government or state-owned enterprise, and the controlling entity is called its parent (or the parent company.) The reason for this distinction is that a lone company cannot be a _____ of any organization; only an entity representing a legal fiction as a separate entity can be a _____.
    a. 1990 Clean Air Act
    b. 33 Strategies of War
    c. 28-hour day
    d. Subsidiary

14. _____ is a costing model that identifies activities in an organization and assigns the cost of each activity resource to all products and services according to the actual consumption by each: it assigns more indirect costs (overhead) into direct costs.

In this way an organization can establish the true cost of its individual products and services for the purposes of identifying and eliminating those which are unprofitable and lowering the prices of those which are overpriced.

In a business organization, the ABC methodology assigns an organization's resource costs through activities to the products and services provided to its customers.

    a. A Stake in the Outcome
    b. Indirect costs
    c. A4e
    d. Activity-based costing

15. _____ are costs that are not directly accountable to a particular function or product. _____ may be either fixed or variable. _____ include taxes, administration, personnel and security costs, and are also known as overhead.
    a. A4e
    b. A Stake in the Outcome
    c. Activity-based management
    d. Indirect costs

16. In business, overhead, _____ or overhead expense refers to an ongoing expense of operating a business. The term overhead is usually used to group expenses that are necessary to the continued functioning of the business, but do not directly generate profits.

Overhead expenses are all costs on the income statement except for direct labor and direct materials.

a. Intangible assets
c. Overhead cost
b. Industrial market segmentation
d. Interlocking directorate

17. In financial accounting, _____ or cost of sales includes the direct costs attributable to the production of the goods sold by a company. This amount includes the materials cost used in creating the goods along with the direct labour costs used to produce the good. It excludes indirect expenses such as distribution costs and sales force costs.
   a. 28-hour day
   c. Reorder point
   b. 1990 Clean Air Act
   d. Cost of goods sold

18. _____ is an adverb or adjective, meaning in proportion. The term is used in many legal and economic contexts, and sometimes spelled pro-rata.

More specifically, _____ means:

1. In proportion to some factor that can be exactly calculated.
2. To count based on amount of time that has passed out of the total time.
3. Proportional Ratio

Pro-rata has a Latin etymology, from pro, according to, for, or by, and rata, feminine ablative of calculated.

Examples in law and economics include the following noted below.

   a. 33 Strategies of War
   c. 1990 Clean Air Act
   b. 28-hour day
   d. Pro rata

19. In management accounting, _____ establishes budget and actual cost of operations, processes, departments or product and the analysis of variances, profitability or social use of funds. Managers use _____ to support decision-making to cut a company's costs and improve profitability. As a form of management accounting, _____ need not follow standards such as GAAP, because its primary use is for internal managers, rather than outside users, and what to compute is instead decided pragmatically.
   a. Marginal cost
   c. Transaction cost
   b. Cost Accounting
   d. Quality costs

20. In economics, the _____ is the theory that the price of an object or condition is determined by the sum of the cost of the resources that went into making it. The cost can compose any of the factors of production (including labour, capital, or land) and taxation.

The theory makes the most sense under assumptions of constant returns to scale and the existence of just one non-produced factor of production.

   a. 33 Strategies of War
   c. 28-hour day
   b. Cost-of-production theory of value
   d. 1990 Clean Air Act

21. _____ is the difference between the revenues earned from and the costs associated with the customer relationship in a specified period.

Chapter 3. Cost Accumulation for Job-Shop and Batch Production Operations

According to Philip Kotler,'a profitable customer is a person, household or a company that overtime, yields a revenue stream that exceeds by an acceptable amount the company's cost stream of attracting, selling and servicing the customer'

Although _____ is nothing more than the result of applying the business concept of profit to a customer relationship, measuring the profitability of a firm's customers or customer groups can often deliver useful business insights.

Quite often a very small percentage of the firm's best customers will account for a large portion of firm profit.

- a. Factory overhead
- c. Profit center
- b. Process costing
- d. Customer profitability

22. _____ is one of the four elements of marketing mix. An organization or set of organizations (go-betweens) involved in the process of making a product or service available for use or consumption by a consumer or business user.

The other three parts of the marketing mix are product, pricing, and promotion.

- a. Missing completely at random
- c. Distribution
- b. Job creation programs
- d. Matching theory

23. _____ is an advertisement in which a particular product specifically mentions a competitor by name for the express purpose of showing why the competitor is inferior to the product naming it.

This should not be confused with parody advertisements, where a fictional product is being advertised for the purpose of poking fun at the particular advertisement, nor should it be confused with the use of a coined brand name for the purpose of comparing the product without actually naming an actual competitor. ('Wikipedia tastes better and is less filling than the Encyclopedia Galactica.')

In the 1980s, during what has been referred to as the cola wars, soft-drink manufacturer Pepsi ran a series of advertisements where people, caught on hidden camera, in a blind taste test, chose Pepsi over rival Coca-Cola.

- a. 28-hour day
- c. 1990 Clean Air Act
- b. Comparative advertising
- d. 33 Strategies of War

24. _____ refers to the structured transmission of data between organizations by electronic means. It is used to transfer electronic documents from one computer system to another (ie) from one trading partner to another trading partner. It is more than mere E-mail; for instance, organizations might replace bills of lading and even checks with appropriate _____ messages.
- a. A Stake in the Outcome
- c. A4e
- b. AAAI
- d. Electronic data interchange

Chapter 3. Cost Accumulation for Job-Shop and Batch Production Operations

25. A _____ is the system of organizations, people, technology, activities, information and resources involved in moving a product or service from supplier to customer. _____ activities transform natural resources, raw materials and components into a finished product that is delivered to the end customer. In sophisticated _____ systems, used products may re-enter the _____ at any point where residual value is recyclable.
  a. Wholesalers
  b. Drop shipping
  c. Packaging
  d. Supply chain

26. _____ is the management of a network of interconnected businesses involved in the ultimate provision of product and service packages required by end customers (Harland, 1996.) _____ spans all movement and storage of raw materials, work-in-process inventory, and finished goods from point of origin to point of consumption (supply chain.)

The definition an American professional association put forward is that _____ encompasses the planning and management of all activities involved in sourcing, procurement, conversion, and logistics management activities.

  a. Freight forwarder
  b. Supply chain management
  c. Drop shipping
  d. Packaging

27. _____ is defined as excess of actual cost over budget. _____ is also sometimes called 'cost escalation,' 'cost increase,' or 'budget overrun.' However, cost escalation and increases do not necessarily result in _____s if cost escalation is included in the budget.

_____ is common in infrastructure, building, and technology projects.

  a. Quality costs
  b. Cost of quality
  c. Transaction cost
  d. Cost overrun

28. _____ generally refers to a list of all planned expenses and revenues. It is a plan for saving and spending. A _____ is an important concept in microeconomics, which uses a _____ line to illustrate the trade-offs between two or more goods.
  a. 33 Strategies of War
  b. 1990 Clean Air Act
  c. 28-hour day
  d. Budget

29. A _____ is a type of bar chart that illustrates a project schedule. _____s illustrate the start and finish dates of the terminal elements and summary elements of a project. Terminal elements and summary elements comprise the work breakdown structure of the project.
  a. 28-hour day
  b. Gantt chart
  c. 1990 Clean Air Act
  d. 33 Strategies of War

30. _____ can be regarded as an outcome of mental processes (cognitive process) leading to the selection of a course of action among several alternatives. Every _____ process produces a final choice. The output can be an action or an opinion of choice.
  a. 33 Strategies of War
  b. 1990 Clean Air Act
  c. Decision making
  d. 28-hour day

31. _____ was a writer, management consultant, and self-described 'social ecologist.' Widely considered to be 'the father of modern management,' his 39 books and countless scholarly and popular articles explored how humans are organized across all sectors of society--in business, government and the nonprofit world. His writings have predicted many of the major developments of the late twentieth century, including privatization and decentralization; the rise of Japan to economic world power; the decisive importance of marketing; and the emergence of the information society with its necessity of lifelong learning. In 1959, Drucker coined the term 'knowledge worker' and later in his life considered knowledge work productivity to be the next frontier of management.

   a. Chrissie Hynde
   b. Peter Ferdinand Drucker
   c. Jacques Al-Salawat Nasruddin Nasser
   d. Debora L. Spar

32. _____ is a process of attributing cost to particular cost centres. For example the wage of the driver of the purchasing department can be allocated to the purchasing department cost centre. It is not necessary to share the wage cost over several different cost centers.cost and services are not identical to each other.

   a. Cost overrun
   b. Fixed costs
   c. Cost accounting
   d. Cost allocation

Chapter 4. Activity-Based Costing Systems

1. In finance, an _____ is a contract between a buyer and a seller that gives the buyer the right--but not the obligation-- to buy or to sell a particular asset (the underlying asset) at a later day at an agreed price. In return for granting the _____, the seller collects a payment (the premium) from the buyer. A call _____ gives the buyer the right to buy the underlying asset; a put _____ gives the buyer of the _____ the right to sell the underlying asset.
   a. A4e
   b. A Stake in the Outcome
   c. AAAI
   d. Option

2. Total _____ is a method of Accounting cost which entails the full cost of manufacturing or providing a service. This includes not just the costs of materials and labour, but also of all manufacturing overheads (whether 'fixed' or 'variable'.) One of the main reasons for absorbing overheads into the cost of units is for inventory valuation purposes.
   a. A4e
   b. AAAI
   c. Absorption costing
   d. A Stake in the Outcome

3. _____ is a costing model that identifies activities in an organization and assigns the cost of each activity resource to all products and services according to the actual consumption by each: it assigns more indirect costs (overhead) into direct costs.

   In this way an organization can establish the true cost of its individual products and services for the purposes of identifying and eliminating those which are unprofitable and lowering the prices of those which are overpriced.

   In a business organization, the ABC methodology assigns an organization's resource costs through activities to the products and services provided to its customers.

   a. A4e
   b. Indirect costs
   c. A Stake in the Outcome
   d. Activity-based costing

4. _____ are costs that are not directly accountable to a particular function or product. _____ may be either fixed or variable. _____ include taxes, administration, personnel and security costs, and are also known as overhead.
   a. Activity-based management
   b. Indirect costs
   c. A4e
   d. A Stake in the Outcome

5. In economics, business, retail, and accounting, a _____ is the value of money that has been used up to produce something, and hence is not available for use anymore. In economics, a _____ is an alternative that is given up as a result of a decision. In business, the _____ may be one of acquisition, in which case the amount of money expended to acquire it is counted as _____.
   a. Cost
   b. Fixed costs
   c. Cost allocation
   d. Cost overrun

6. _____ is a process of attributing cost to particular cost centres. For example the wage of the driver of the purchasing department can be allocated to the purchasing department cost centre. It is not necessary to share the wage cost over several different cost centers.cost and services are not identical to each other.
   a. Fixed costs
   b. Cost overrun
   c. Cost accounting
   d. Cost allocation

Chapter 4. Activity-Based Costing Systems

7. _____ is an increasingly broadening term with which an organization, or other human system describes the combination of traditionally administrative personnel functions with acquisition and application of skills, knowledge and experience, Employee Relations and resource planning at various levels. The field draws upon concepts developed in Industrial/Organizational Psychology and System Theory. _____ has at least two related interpretations depending on context. The original usage derives from political economy and economics, where it was traditionally called labor, one of four factors of production although this perspective is changing as a function of new and ongoing research into more strategic approaches at national levels. This first usage is used more in terms of '_____ development', and can go beyond just organizations to the level of nations . The more traditional usage within corporations and businesses refers to the individuals within a firm or agency, and to the portion of the organization that deals with hiring, firing, training, and other personnel issues, typically referred to as `_____ management'.

   a. Human resource management   b. Progressive discipline
   c. Bradford Factor   d. Human resources

8. A _____ is essentially breaking down a system to gain insight into its compositional sub-systems. In a _____ an overview of the system is first formulated, specifying but not detailing any first-level subsystems. Each subsystem is then refined in yet greater detail, sometimes in many additional subsystem levels, until the entire specification is reduced to base elements.

   a. 33 Strategies of War   b. 28-hour day
   c. Top-down approach   d. 1990 Clean Air Act

9. The phrase mergers and _____s refers to the aspect of corporate strategy, corporate finance and management dealing with the buying, selling and combining of different companies that can aid, finance, or help a growing company in a given industry grow rapidly without having to create another business entity.

An _____, also known as a takeover or a buyout, is the buying of one company (the 'target') by another. An _____ may be friendly or hostile.

   a. A4e   b. A Stake in the Outcome
   c. AAAI   d. Acquisition

10. _____ is the difference between the revenues earned from and the costs associated with the customer relationship in a specified period.

According to Philip Kotler,'a profitable customer is a person, household or a company that overtime, yields a revenue stream that exceeds by an acceptable amount the company's cost stream of attracting, selling and servicing the customer'

Although _____ is nothing more than the result of applying the business concept of profit to a customer relationship, measuring the profitability of a firm's customers or customer groups can often deliver useful business insights.

Quite often a very small percentage of the firm's best customers will account for a large portion of firm profit.

   a. Customer profitability   b. Process costing
   c. Factory overhead   d. Profit center

11. _____ is an advertisement in which a particular product specifically mentions a competitor by name for the express purpose of showing why the competitor is inferior to the product naming it.

This should not be confused with parody advertisements, where a fictional product is being advertised for the purpose of poking fun at the particular advertisement, nor should it be confused with the use of a coined brand name for the purpose of comparing the product without actually naming an actual competitor. ('Wikipedia tastes better and is less filling than the Encyclopedia Galactica.')

In the 1980s, during what has been referred to as the cola wars, soft-drink manufacturer Pepsi ran a series of advertisements where people, caught on hidden camera, in a blind taste test, chose Pepsi over rival Coca-Cola.

- a. 28-hour day
- b. 33 Strategies of War
- c. 1990 Clean Air Act
- d. Comparative advertising

12. _____ is the process whereby an organization establishes the parameters within which programs, investments, and acquisitions are reaching the desired results. Performance Reference Model of the Federal Enterprise Architecture, 2005.

This process of measuring performance often requires the use of statistical evidence to determine progress toward specific defined organizational objectives.

There are many types of measurements.

- a. Workflow
- b. CIFMS
- c. Crisis management
- d. Performance measurement

13. The _____ of a product is the cost per standard unit supplied, which may be a single sample or a container of a given number. When purchasing more than a single unit, the total cost will increase with the number of units, but it is common for the _____ to decrease as quantity is increased (bulk purchasing), as there are discounts etc. This reduction in long run _____s which arise from an increase in production/purchasing is due to the fixed costs being spread out over more products and is called economies of scale.

- a. AAAI
- b. A4e
- c. A Stake in the Outcome
- d. Unit cost

14. A _____ is a process in which a potential employee is evaluated by an employer for prospective employment in their company, organization and was established in the late 16th century.

A _____ typically precedes the hiring decision, and is used to evaluate the candidate. The interview is usually preceded by the evaluation of submitted résumés from interested candidates, then selecting a small number of candidates for interviews.

- a. Payrolling
- b. Supported employment
- c. Split shift
- d. Job interview

Chapter 5. Activity-Based Management

1. _____ is a method of identifying and evaluating activities that a business performs using activity-based costing to carry out a value chain analysis or a re-engineering initiative to improve strategic and operational decisions in an organization. Activity-based costing establishes relationships between overhead costs and activities so that overhead costs can be more precisely allocated to products, services, or customer segments. _____ focuses on managing activities to reduce costs and improve customer value.
   a. A Stake in the Outcome
   b. A4e
   c. Indirect costs
   d. Activity-based management

2. _____ is a costing model that identifies activities in an organization and assigns the cost of each activity resource to all products and services according to the actual consumption by each: it assigns more indirect costs (overhead) into direct costs.

   In this way an organization can establish the true cost of its individual products and services for the purposes of identifying and eliminating those which are unprofitable and lowering the prices of those which are overpriced.

   In a business organization, the ABC methodology assigns an organization's resource costs through activities to the products and services provided to its customers.

   a. Activity-based costing
   b. A4e
   c. Indirect costs
   d. A Stake in the Outcome

3. In organizational development (OD), _____ is a series of actions taken by a Process Owner to identify, analyze and improve existing processes within an organization to meet new goals and objectives. These actions often follow a specific methodology or strategy to create successful results. A sampling of these are listed below.
   a. Product innovation
   b. Process improvement
   c. Letter of resignation
   d. Supervisory board

4. _____ is a pricing method used by firms. It is defined as 'a cost management tool for reducing the overall cost of a product over its entire life-cycle with the help of production, engineering, research and design'. A target cost is the maximum amount of cost that can be incurred on a product and with it the firm can still earn the required profit margin from that product at a particular selling price.
   a. Price war
   b. Pricing
   c. Pricing objectives
   d. Target costing

5. In economics, business, retail, and accounting, a _____ is the value of money that has been used up to produce something, and hence is not available for use anymore. In economics, a _____ is an alternative that is given up as a result of a decision. In business, the _____ may be one of acquisition, in which case the amount of money expended to acquire it is counted as _____.
   a. Cost overrun
   b. Cost allocation
   c. Fixed costs
   d. Cost

6. In business, operating margin, operating income margin, operating profit margin or _____ is the ratio of operating income (operating profit in the UK) divided by net sales, usually presented in percent.

(Relevant figures in italics)

It is a measurement of what proportion of a company's revenue is left over, before taxes and other indirect costs (such as rent, bonus, interest, etc.), after paying for variable costs of production as wages, raw materials, etc. A good operating margin is needed for a company to be able to pay for its fixed costs, such as interest on debt.

a. Rate of return	b. Return on sales
c. P/E ratio	d. Return on equity

7. The _____ is a concept from business management that was first described and popularized by Michael Porter in his 1985 best-seller, Competitive Advantage: Creating and Sustaining Superior Performance.

A _____ is a chain of activities. Products pass through all activities of the chain in order and at each activity the product gains some value. The chain of activities gives the products more added value than the sum of added values of all activities. It is important not to mix the concept of the _____ with the costs occurring throughout the activities.

a. Customer relationship management	b. Market development
c. Mass marketing	d. Value chain

8. _____ refers to the difference between the cost of materials purchased by a company plus the cost of the labor to assemble a product and the price at which the company sells the product. An example is the price of gasoline at the pump over the price of the oil in it. In national accounts used in macroeconomics, it refers to the contribution of the factors of production, i.e., land, labor, and capital goods, to raising the value of a product and corresponds to the incomes received by the owners of these factors.

a. Deregulation	b. Value added
c. Rehn-Meidner Model	d. Minimum wage

9. _____ is a concept in economics which refers to the extent to which an enterprise or a nation actually uses its installed productive capacity. Thus, it refers to the relationship between actual output that 'is' produced with the installed equipment and the potential output which 'could' be produced with it, if capacity was fully used.

If market demand grows, _____ will rise.

a. Factors of production	b. Multifactor productivity
c. Capacity utilization	d. Diseconomies of scale

10. In queueing theory, _____ is the proportion of the system's resources which is used by the traffic which arrives at it. It should be strictly less than one for the system to function well. It is usually represented by the symbol ρ.

a. Utilization	b. AAAI
c. A4e	d. A Stake in the Outcome

11. _____ describes types of employment in which a worker is paid a fixed 'piece rate' for each unit produced or action performed. _____ is also a form of performance-related pay (PRP) and is the oldest form of performance pay.

In a manufacturing setting, the output of piece work can be measured by the number of physical items (pieces) produced, such as when a garment worker is paid per operational step completed, regardless of the time required.

- a. Methods-time measurement
- b. Capacity planning
- c. Piecework
- d. Productivity

12. A _____ is a group of employees from various functional areas of the organization - research, engineering, marketing, finance. human resources, and operations, for example - who are all focused on a specific objective and are responsible to work as a team to improve coordination and innovation across divisions and resolve mutual problems.
- a. Sociotechnical systems
- b. Graduate recruitment
- c. Goal-setting theory
- d. Cross-functional team

13. _____ is an idea in the field of Organizational studies and management which describes the psychology, attitudes, experiences, beliefs and Values (personal and cultural values) of an organization. It has been defined as 'the specific collection of values and norms that are shared by people and groups in an organization and that control the way they interact with each other and with stakeholders outside the organization.'

This definition continues to explain organizational values also known as 'beliefs and ideas about what kinds of goals members of an organization should pursue and ideas about the appropriate kinds or standards of behavior organizational members should use to achieve these goals. From organizational values develop organizational norms, guidelines or expectations that prescribe appropriate kinds of behavior by employees in particular situations and control the behavior of organizational members towards one another.'

_____ is not the same as corporate culture.

- a. Organizational culture
- b. Union shop
- c. Organizational development
- d. Organizational effectiveness

14. _____ generally refers to a list of all planned expenses and revenues. It is a plan for saving and spending. A _____ is an important concept in microeconomics, which uses a _____ line to illustrate the trade-offs between two or more goods.
- a. 33 Strategies of War
- b. 28-hour day
- c. Budget
- d. 1990 Clean Air Act

15. _____ refers to the movement of cash into or out of a business or financial product. It is usually measured during a specified, finite period of time. Measurement of _____ can be used

- to determine a project's rate of return or value. The time of _____s into and out of projects are used as inputs in financial models such as internal rate of return, and net present value.
- to determine problems with a business's liquidity. Being profitable does not necessarily mean being liquid. A company can fail because of a shortage of cash, even while profitable.
- as an alternate measure of a business's profits when it is believed that accrual accounting concepts do not represent economic realities. For example, a company may be notionally profitable but generating little operational cash (as may be the case for a company that barters its products rather than selling for cash.) In such a case, the company may be deriving additional operating cash by issuing shares evaluating default risk, re-investment requirements, etc.

_____ is a generic term used differently depending on the context. It may be defined by users for their own purposes.

a. Gross profit margin
b. Sweat equity
c. Gross profit
d. Cash flow

Chapter 6. Managing Customer Profitability

1. _____ is a term that refers both to:

   - a formal discipline used to help appraise, or assess, the case for a project or proposal, which itself is a process known as project appraisal; and
   - an informal approach to making decisions of any kind.

Under both definitions the process involves, whether explicitly or implicitly, weighing the total expected costs against the total expected benefits of one or more actions in order to choose the best or most profitable option. The formal process is often referred to as either CBA (_____) or BCost-benefit analysis

A hallmark of CBA is that all benefits and all costs are expressed in money terms, and are adjusted for the time value of money, so that all flows of benefits and flows of project costs over time (which tend to occur at different points in time) are expressed on a common basis in terms of their 'present value.' Closely related, but slightly different, formal techniques include Cost-effectiveness analysis, Economic impact analysis, Fiscal impact analysis and Social Return on Investment(SROI) analysis. The latter builds upon the logic of _____, but differs in that it is explicitly designed to inform the practical decision-making of enterprise managers and investors focused on optimising their social and environmental impacts.

   a. Gittins index
   b. Cost-benefit analysis
   c. Kepner-Tregoe
   d. Decision engineering

2. _____ is the difference between the revenues earned from and the costs associated with the customer relationship in a specified period.

According to Philip Kotler,'a profitable customer is a person, household or a company that overtime, yields a revenue stream that exceeds by an acceptable amount the company's cost stream of attracting, selling and servicing the customer'

Although _____ is nothing more than the result of applying the business concept of profit to a customer relationship, measuring the profitability of a firm's customers or customer groups can often deliver useful business insights.

Quite often a very small percentage of the firm's best customers will account for a large portion of firm profit.

   a. Factory overhead
   b. Profit center
   c. Process costing
   d. Customer profitability

3. In business, operating margin, operating income margin, operating profit margin or _____ is the ratio of operating income (operating profit in the UK) divided by net sales, usually presented in percent.

>

(Relevant figures in italics)

It is a measurement of what proportion of a company's revenue is left over, before taxes and other indirect costs (such as rent, bonus, interest, etc.), after paying for variable costs of production as wages, raw materials, etc. A good operating margin is needed for a company to be able to pay for its fixed costs, such as interest on debt.

a. P/E ratio
b. Rate of return
c. Return on sales
d. Return on equity

4. A _____ is a special type of bar chart where the values being plotted are arranged in descending order. The graph is accompanied by a line graph which shows the cumulative totals of each category, left to right. The chart was named for Vilfredo Pareto.

a. Pareto chart
b. 1990 Clean Air Act
c. 33 Strategies of War
d. 28-hour day

5. There are many important decisions about product and service development and marketing. In the process of product development and marketing we should focus on strategic decisions about product attributes, product branding, product packaging, product labeling and product support services. But product strategy also calls for building a _____.

a. Product bundling
b. Marketing strategy
c. Context analysis
d. Product line

6. In economics, business, retail, and accounting, a _____ is the value of money that has been used up to produce something, and hence is not available for use anymore. In economics, a _____ is an alternative that is given up as a result of a decision. In business, the _____ may be one of acquisition, in which case the amount of money expended to acquire it is counted as _____.

a. Cost
b. Fixed costs
c. Cost overrun
d. Cost allocation

7. _____, a business term, is a measure of how products and services supplied by a company meet or surpass customer expectation. It is seen as a key performance indicator within business and is part of the four perspectives of a Balanced Scorecard.

In a competitive marketplace where businesses compete for customers, _____ is seen as a key differentiator and increasingly has become a key element of business strategy.

a. Horizontal integration
b. Critical Success Factor
c. Foreign ownership
d. Customer satisfaction

8. _____ is an advertisement in which a particular product specifically mentions a competitor by name for the express purpose of showing why the competitor is inferior to the product naming it.

Chapter 6. Managing Customer Profitability

This should not be confused with parody advertisements, where a fictional product is being advertised for the purpose of poking fun at the particular advertisement, nor should it be confused with the use of a coined brand name for the purpose of comparing the product without actually naming an actual competitor. ('Wikipedia tastes better and is less filling than the Encyclopedia Galactica.')

In the 1980s, during what has been referred to as the cola wars, soft-drink manufacturer Pepsi ran a series of advertisements where people, caught on hidden camera, in a blind taste test, chose Pepsi over rival Coca-Cola.

a. 1990 Clean Air Act
b. Comparative advertising
c. 28-hour day
d. 33 Strategies of War

9. _____ refers to the movement of cash into or out of a business or financial product. It is usually measured during a specified, finite period of time. Measurement of _____ can be used

- to determine a project's rate of return or value. The time of _____s into and out of projects are used as inputs in financial models such as internal rate of return, and net present value.
- to determine problems with a business's liquidity. Being profitable does not necessarily mean being liquid. A company can fail because of a shortage of cash, even while profitable.
- as an alternate measure of a business's profits when it is believed that accrual accounting concepts do not represent economic realities. For example, a company may be notionally profitable but generating little operational cash (as may be the case for a company that barters its products rather than selling for cash.) In such a case, the company may be deriving additional operating cash by issuing shares evaluating default risk, re-investment requirements, etc.

_____ is a generic term used differently depending on the context. It may be defined by users for their own purposes.

a. Gross profit
b. Gross profit margin
c. Sweat equity
d. Cash flow

10. In cost-volume-profit analysis, a form of management accounting, _____ is the marginal profit per unit sale. It is a useful quantity in carrying out various calculations, and can be used as a measure of operating leverage.

The Total _____ is Total Revenue (TR, or Sales) minus Total Variable Cost (TVC):

TContribution margin = TR − TVC

The Unit _____ (C) is Unit Revenue (Price, P) minus Unit Variable Cost (V):

$C = P - V$

Chapter 6. Managing Customer Profitability

The _____ Ratio is the percentage of Contribution over Total Revenue, which can be calculated from the unit contribution over unit price or total contribution over Total Revenue:

$$\frac{C}{P} = \frac{P-V}{P} = \frac{\text{Unit Contribution Margin}}{\text{Price}} = \frac{\text{Total Contribution Margin}}{\text{Total Revenue}}$$

For instance, if the price is $10 and the unit variable cost is $2, then the unit _____ is $8, and the _____ ratio is $8/$10 = 80%.

- a. Profit center
- b. Contribution margin
- c. Factory overhead
- d. Customer profitability

11. In financial accounting, _____ or cost of sales includes the direct costs attributable to the production of the goods sold by a company. This amount includes the materials cost used in creating the goods along with the direct labour costs used to produce the good. It excludes indirect expenses such as distribution costs and sales force costs.
- a. Reorder point
- b. Cost of goods sold
- c. 28-hour day
- d. 1990 Clean Air Act

12. _____ is one of the four elements of marketing mix. An organization or set of organizations (go-betweens) involved in the process of making a product or service available for use or consumption by a consumer or business user.

The other three parts of the marketing mix are product, pricing, and promotion.

- a. Matching theory
- b. Missing completely at random
- c. Job creation programs
- d. Distribution

13. _____ is an integrated communications-based process through which individuals and communities discover that existing and newly-identified needs and wants may be satisfied by the products and services of others.

_____ is defined by the American _____ Association as the activity, set of institutions, and processes for creating, communicating, delivering, and exchanging offerings that have value for customers, clients, partners, and society at large. The term developed from the original meaning which referred literally to going to market, as in shopping, or going to a market to buy or sell goods or services.

- a. Market development
- b. Marketing
- c. Customer relationship management
- d. Disruptive technology

14. A sample is a subject chosen from a population for investigation. A _____ is one chosen by a method involving an unpredictable component. Random sampling can also refer to taking a number of independent observations from the same probability distribution, without involving any real population.
- a. Random sample
- b. 28-hour day
- c. 1990 Clean Air Act
- d. 33 Strategies of War

Chapter 6. Managing Customer Profitability

15. The phrase _____, according to the Organization for Economic Co-operation and Development, refers to 'creative work undertaken on a systematic basis in order to increase the stock of knowledge, including knowledge of man, culture and society, and the use of this stock of knowledge to devise new applications [sic]'

New product design and development is more than often a crucial factor in the survival of a company. In an industry that is fast changing, firms must continually revise their design and range of products. This is necessary due to continuous technology change and development as well as other competitors and the changing preference of customers.

   a. 33 Strategies of War
   c. 1990 Clean Air Act
   b. 28-hour day
   d. Research and development

16. _____ is subcontracting a process, such as product design or manufacturing, to a third-party company. The decision to outsource is often made in the interest of lowering cost or making better use of time and energy costs, redirecting or conserving energy directed at the competencies of a particular business, or to make more efficient use of land, labor, capital, (information) technology and resources. _____ became part of the business lexicon during the 1980s.
   a. Operant conditioning
   c. Unemployment insurance
   b. Opinion leadership
   d. Outsourcing

17. In the fields of science, engineering, industry and statistics, _____ is the degree of closeness of a measured or calculated quantity to its actual (true) value. _____ is closely related to precision, also called reproducibility or repeatability, the degree to which further measurements or calculations show the same or similar results. _____ indicates proximity to the true value, precision to the repeatability or reproducibility of the measurement

The results of calculations or a measurement can be accurate but not precise, precise but not accurate, neither, or both.

   a. Accuracy
   c. A4e
   b. AAAI
   d. A Stake in the Outcome

18. _____ is a company's financial statement that indicates how the revenue is transformed into the net income The purpose of the _____ is to show managers and investors whether the company made or lost money during the period being reported.

The important thing to remember about an _____ is that it represents a period of time.

   a. A Stake in the Outcome
   c. A4e
   b. AAAI
   d. Income statement

19. _____ are formal records of the financial activities of a business, person, or other entity. In British English, including United Kingdom company law, _____ are often referred to as accounts, although the term _____ is also used, particularly by accountants.

_____ provide an overview of a business or person's financial condition in both short and long term.

a. 33 Strategies of War
c. 1990 Clean Air Act
b. 28-hour day
d. Financial statements

20. _____ is a term used to describe the efforts made by a downsizing company to help its redundant employees through the redundancy transition and help them re-orientate to the job market. A consultancy firm usually provides the _____ services. This is achieved through practical and psychological support.

a. Unemployment benefits
c. Unemployment compensation
b. Unemployment Provision Convention, 1934
d. Outplacement

21. _____ is the provision of service to customers before, during and after a purchase.

According to Turban et al. (2002), '_____ is a series of activities designed to enhance the level of customer satisfaction - that is, the feeling that a product or service has met the customer expectation.'

Its importance varies by product, industry and customer; defective or broken merchandise can be exchanged, often only with a receipt and within a specified time frame.

a. Service rate
c. 28-hour day
b. Customer service
d. 1990 Clean Air Act

Chapter 7. Managing Quality and Time to Create Value

1. The _____ of a company or public agency is the corporate officer primarily responsible for managing the financial risks of the business or agency. This officer is also responsible for financial planning and record-keeping, as well as financial reporting to higher management. (In recent years, however, the role has expanded to encompass communicating financial performance and forecasts to the analyst community.)
   a. 1990 Clean Air Act
   b. 33 Strategies of War
   c. Chief financial officer
   d. 28-hour day

2. A _____ is a special type of bar chart where the values being plotted are arranged in descending order. The graph is accompanied by a line graph which shows the cumulative totals of each category, left to right. The chart was named for Vilfredo Pareto.
   a. 28-hour day
   b. Pareto chart
   c. 33 Strategies of War
   d. 1990 Clean Air Act

3. _____ is a business management strategy aimed at embedding awareness of quality in all organizational processes. _____ has been widely used in manufacturing, education, hospitals, call centers, government, and service industries, as well as NASA space and science programs.

   As defined by the International Organization for Standardization (ISO):

   '_____ is a management approach for an organization, centered on quality, based on the participation of all its members and aiming at long-term success through customer satisfaction, and benefits to all members of the organization and to society.' ISO 8402:1994

   One major aim is to reduce variation from every process so that greater consistency of effort is obtained. (Royse, D., Thyer, B., Padgett D., ' Logan T., 2006)

   a. Total quality management
   b. Quality management
   c. 28-hour day
   d. 1990 Clean Air Act

4. In economics, business, retail, and accounting, a _____ is the value of money that has been used up to produce something, and hence is not available for use anymore. In economics, a _____ is an alternative that is given up as a result of a decision. In business, the _____ may be one of acquisition, in which case the amount of money expended to acquire it is counted as _____.
   a. Cost
   b. Cost overrun
   c. Fixed costs
   d. Cost allocation

5. _____ can be considered to have three main components: quality control, quality assurance and quality improvement. _____ is focused not only on product quality, but also the means to achieve it. _____ therefore uses quality assurance and control of processes as well as products to achieve more consistent quality.
   a. 1990 Clean Air Act
   b. Quality management
   c. 28-hour day
   d. Total quality management

6. _____ is the provision of service to customers before, during and after a purchase.

According to Turban et al. (2002), '_____ is a series of activities designed to enhance the level of customer satisfaction - that is, the feeling that a product or service has met the customer expectation.'

Its importance varies by product, industry and customer; defective or broken merchandise can be exchanged, often only with a receipt and within a specified time frame.

- a. Service rate
- b. 1990 Clean Air Act
- c. 28-hour day
- d. Customer service

7. In economics and finance, _____ is the change in total cost that arises when the quantity produced changes by one unit. It is the cost of producing one more unit of a good. Mathematically, the _____ function is expressed as the first derivative of the total cost (TC) function with respect to quantity (Q.)
- a. Variable cost
- b. Cost overrun
- c. Transaction cost
- d. Marginal cost

8. _____ is an advertisement in which a particular product specifically mentions a competitor by name for the express purpose of showing why the competitor is inferior to the product naming it.

This should not be confused with parody advertisements, where a fictional product is being advertised for the purpose of poking fun at the particular advertisement, nor should it be confused with the use of a coined brand name for the purpose of comparing the product without actually naming an actual competitor. ('Wikipedia tastes better and is less filling than the Encyclopedia Galactica.')

In the 1980s, during what has been referred to as the cola wars, soft-drink manufacturer Pepsi ran a series of advertisements where people, caught on hidden camera, in a blind taste test, chose Pepsi over rival Coca-Cola.

- a. 1990 Clean Air Act
- b. 33 Strategies of War
- c. 28-hour day
- d. Comparative advertising

9. A _____ shows us a summarized grouping of data divided into mutually exclusive classes and the number of occurrences in a class. It is a way of showing unorganized data e.g. to show results of an election, income of people for a certain region, sales of a product within a certain period, student loan amounts of graduates, etc. Some of the graphs that can be used with _____s are histograms, line graphs, bar charts and pie charts.
- a. Frequency distribution
- b. Homoscedastic
- c. Statistics
- d. Statistically significant

10. In statistics, a _____ is a graphical display of tabulated frequencies, shown as bars. It shows what proportion of cases fall into each of several categories: it is a form of data binning. The categories are usually specified as non-overlapping intervals of some variable.
- a. Correlation
- b. Histogram
- c. Statistics
- d. Standard deviation

11. In economics, _____s are key economic variables that economists used to predict a new phase of the business cycle. A _____ is one that changes before the economy does; a lagging indicator is one that changes after the economy has changed. Examples of _____s include stock prices, which often improve or worsen before a similar change in the economy.

Chapter 7. Managing Quality and Time to Create Value

a. Leading indicator
b. Perfect competition
c. Human capital
d. Deflation

12. _____ is one of the four elements of marketing mix. An organization or set of organizations (go-betweens) involved in the process of making a product or service available for use or consumption by a consumer or business user.

The other three parts of the marketing mix are product, pricing, and promotion.

a. Matching theory
b. Distribution
c. Job creation programs
d. Missing completely at random

13. _____ is one of the managerial functions like planning, organizing, staffing and directing. It is an important function because it helps to check the errors and to take the corrective action so that deviation from standards are minimized and stated goals of the organization are achieved in desired manner. According to modern concepts, _____ is a foreseeing action whereas earlier concept of _____ was used only when errors were detected. _____ in management means setting standards, measuring actual performance and taking corrective action.

a. Turnover
b. Control
c. Decision tree pruning
d. Schedule of reinforcement

14. The _____ in statistical process control is a tool used to determine whether a manufacturing or business process is in a state of statistical control or not.

If the chart indicates that the process is currently under control then it can be used with confidence to predict the future performance of the process. If the chart indicates that the process being monitored is not in control, the pattern it reveals can help determine the source of variation to be eliminated to bring the process back into control.

a. Simple moving average
b. Failure rate
c. Time series analysis
d. Control chart

15. A _____, also known as a run-sequence plot is a graph that displays observed data in a time sequence. Often, the data displayed represent some aspect of the output or performance of a manufacturing or other business process.

Run sequence plots are an easy way to graphically summarize a univariate data set.

a. 1990 Clean Air Act
b. 33 Strategies of War
c. 28-hour day
d. Run chart

16. _____ are horizontal lines drawn on an statistical process control chart, usually at a distance of >±3 standard deviations of the plotted statistic from the statistic's mean.

For normally distributed statistics, the area bracketed by the _____ will on average contain 99.73% of all the plot points on the chart, as long as the process is and remains in statistical control.

_____ should not be confused with tolerance limits, which are completely independent of the distribution of the plotted sample statistic.

Chapter 7. Managing Quality and Time to Create Value

a. Skewness risk
c. T-statistic
b. 1990 Clean Air Act
d. Control limits

17. _____ is an increasingly broadening term with which an organization, or other human system describes the combination of traditionally administrative personnel functions with acquisition and application of skills, knowledge and experience, Employee Relations and resource planning at various levels. The field draws upon concepts developed in Industrial/Organizational Psychology and System Theory. _____ has at least two related interpretations depending on context. The original usage derives from political economy and economics, where it was traditionally called labor, one of four factors of production although this perspective is changing as a function of new and ongoing research into more strategic approaches at national levels. This first usage is used more in terms of '_____ development', and can go beyond just organizations to the level of nations. The more traditional usage within corporations and businesses refers to the individuals within a firm or agency, and to the portion of the organization that deals with hiring, firing, training, and other personnel issues, typically referred to as '_____ management'.

a. Human resources
c. Bradford Factor
b. Progressive discipline
d. Human resource management

18. A _____ is a common type of chart, that represents an algorithm or process, showing the steps as boxes of various kinds, and their order by connecting these with arrows. _____s are used in analyzing, designing, documenting or managing a process or program in various fields.

The first structured method for documenting process flow, the 'flow process chart', was introduced by Frank Gilbreth to members of ASME in 1921 as the presentation 'Process Charts--First Steps in Finding the One Best Way'.

a. 33 Strategies of War
c. 28-hour day
b. 1990 Clean Air Act
d. Flowchart

19. A scatter plot is a type of display using Cartesian coordinates to display values for two variables for a set of data.

The data is displayed as a collection of points, each having the value of one variable determining the position on the horizontal axis and the value of the other variable determining the position on the vertical axis. A scatter plot is also called a scatter chart, _____ and scatter graph.

a. 33 Strategies of War
c. 1990 Clean Air Act
b. Scatter diagram
d. 28-hour day

20. _____, a business term, is a measure of how products and services supplied by a company meet or surpass customer expectation. It is seen as a key performance indicator within business and is part of the four perspectives of a Balanced Scorecard.

In a competitive marketplace where businesses compete for customers, _____ is seen as a key differentiator and increasingly has become a key element of business strategy.

a. Horizontal integration
c. Customer satisfaction
b. Foreign ownership
d. Critical Success Factor

21. The concept of quality costs is a means to quantify the total _____-related efforts and deficiencies. It was first described by Armand V. Feigenbaum in a 1956 Harvard Business Review article.

Prior to its introduction, the general perception was that higher quality requires higher costs, either by buying better materials or machines or by hiring more labor.

a. Quality costs
b. Fixed costs
c. Cost accounting
d. Cost of quality

22. _____ can be defined as the idea generation, concept development, testing and manufacturing or implementation of a physical object or service. _____ers conceptualize and evaluate ideas, making them tangible through products in a more systematic approach. The role of a _____er encompasses many characteristics of the marketing manager, product manager, industrial designer and design engineer.
a. Affiliation
b. Adam Smith
c. Abraham Harold Maslow
d. Product design

23. _____ is a 'method to transform user demands into design quality, to deploy the functions forming quality, and to deploy methods for achieving the design quality into subsystems and component parts, and ultimately to specific elements of the manufacturing process.', as described by Dr. Yoji Akao, who originally developed _____ in Japan in 1966, when the author combined his work in quality assurance and quality control points with function deployment used in Value Engineering.

_____ is designed to help planners focus on characteristics of a new or existing product or service from the viewpoints of market segments, company, or technology-development needs. The technique yields graphs and matrices.

a. Hoshin Kanri
b. Quality function deployment
c. Learning organization
d. 1990 Clean Air Act

24. _____ is an effective method of monitoring a process through the use of control charts. Control charts enable the use of objective criteria for distinguishing background variation from events of significance based on statistical techniques. Much of its power lies in the ability to monitor both process center and its variation about that center.
a. Single Minute Exchange of Die
b. Statistical process control
c. Process capability
d. Quality control

25. _____ in mathematics and statistics is concerned with identifying the values, uncertainties and other issues relevant in a given decision and the resulting optimal decision. It is sometimes called game theory.

Most of _____ is normative or prescriptive, i.e., it is concerned with identifying the best decision to take, assuming an ideal decision maker who is fully informed, able to compute with perfect accuracy, and fully rational.

a. Nominal group technique
b. Belief decision matrix
c. Rational planning model
d. Decision theory

Chapter 7. Managing Quality and Time to Create Value

26. _____ is a costing model that identifies activities in an organization and assigns the cost of each activity resource to all products and services according to the actual consumption by each: it assigns more indirect costs (overhead) into direct costs.

In this way an organization can establish the true cost of its individual products and services for the purposes of identifying and eliminating those which are unprofitable and lowering the prices of those which are overpriced.

In a business organization, the ABC methodology assigns an organization's resource costs through activities to the products and services provided to its customers.

a. Activity-based costing
b. A4e
c. Indirect costs
d. A Stake in the Outcome

27. _____ is the area of law in which manufacturers, distributors, suppliers, retailers, and others who make products available to the public are held responsible for the injuries those products cause.

In the United States, the claims most commonly associated with _____ are negligence, strict liability, breach of warranty, and various consumer protection claims. The majority of _____ laws are determined at the state level and vary widely from state to state.

a. Leave of absence
b. Product liability
c. Railway Labor Act
d. Right-to-work laws

28. _____ is fixing any sort of mechanical or electrical device should it become out of order or broken (known as repair, unscheduled or casualty maintenance) as well as performing the routine actions which keep the device in working order (known as scheduled maintenance) or prevent trouble from arising (preventive maintenance.) MRO may be defined as, 'All actions which have the objective of retaining or restoring an item in or to a state in which it can perform its required function. The actions include the combination of all technical and corresponding administrative, managerial, and supervision actions.'

MRO operations can be categorised by whether the product remains the property of the customer, i.e., a service is being offer or whether the product is brought by the reprocessing organisation and sold to any customer wishing to make the purchase.

a. 1990 Clean Air Act
b. 33 Strategies of War
c. 28-hour day
d. Maintenance, repair and operations

29. The _____ is given by the United States National Institute of Standards and Technology. Through the actions of the National Productivity Advisory Committee chaired by Jack Grayson, it was established by the Malcolm Baldrige National Quality Improvement Act of 1987 - Public Law 100-107 and named for Malcolm Baldrige, who served as United States Secretary of Commerce during the Reagan administration from 1981 until his 1987 death in a rodeo accident. APQC, , organized the first White House Conference on Productivity, spearheading the creation and design of the _____ in 1987, and jointly administering the award for its first three years.

a. Time and attendance
b. Business Network Transformation
c. Scenario planning
d. Malcolm Baldrige National Quality Award

Chapter 7. Managing Quality and Time to Create Value

30. _____ refers to a range of skills, tools, and techniques used to manage time when accomplishing specific tasks, projects and goals. This set encompass a wide scope of activities, and these include planning, allocating, setting goals, delegation, analysis of time spent, monitoring, organizing, scheduling, and prioritizing. Initially _____ referred to just business or work activities, but eventually the term broadened to include personal activities also.

   a. Voice of the customer
   b. Formula for Change
   c. Cash cow
   d. Time management

31. In business and engineering, _____ is the term used to describe the complete process of bringing a new product or service to market. There are two parallel paths involved in the _____ process: one involves the idea generation, product design, and detail engineering; the other involves market research and marketing analysis. Companies typically see _____ as the first stage in generating and commercializing new products within the overall strategic process of product life cycle management used to maintain or grow their market share.

   a. 33 Strategies of War
   b. 28-hour day
   c. 1990 Clean Air Act
   d. New product development

32. In business and engineering, new _____ is the term used to describe the complete process of bringing a new product or service to market. There are two parallel paths involved in the NProduct development process: one involves the idea generation, product design, and detail engineering; the other involves market research and marketing analysis. Companies typically see new _____ as the first stage in generating and commercializing new products within the overall strategic process of product life cycle management used to maintain or grow their market share.

   a. 28-hour day
   b. Product development
   c. 1990 Clean Air Act
   d. 33 Strategies of War

33. A _____ or business method is a collection of related, structured activities or tasks that produce a specific service or product (serve a particular goal) for a particular customer or customers. It often can be visualized with a flowchart as a sequence of activities.

There are three types of _____ es:

1. Management processes, the processes that govern the operation of a system. Typical management processes include 'Corporate Governance' and 'Strategic Management'.
2. Operational processes, processes that constitute the core business and create the primary value stream. Typical operational processes are Purchasing, Manufacturing, Marketing, and Sales.
3. Supporting processes, which support the core processes. Examples include Accounting, Recruitment, Technical support.

A _____ begins with a customer's need and ends with a customer's need fulfillment. Process oriented organizations break down the barriers of structural departments and try to avoid functional silos.

   a. 33 Strategies of War
   b. 28-hour day
   c. 1990 Clean Air Act
   d. Business process

34. _____ is, in computer science and management, an approach aiming at improvements by means of elevating efficiency and effectiveness of the business process that exist within and across organizations. The key to _____ is for organizations to look at their business processes from a 'clean slate' perspective and determine how they can best construct these processes to improve how they conduct business. _____ Cycle.

____ is also known as ____, Business Process Redesign, Business Transformation, or Business Process Change Management.

a. Product life cycle
b. Personal management interview
c. Business process reengineering
d. Horizontal integration

35. ____ refers to metrics and measures of output from production processes, per unit of input. Labor ____, for example, is typically measured as a ratio of output per labor-hour, an input. ____ may be conceived of as a metrics of the technical or engineering efficiency of production.

a. Master production schedule
b. Value engineering
c. Productivity
d. Remanufacturing

36. In economics, ____ (TFP) is a variable which accounts for effects in total output not caused by inputs. For example, a year with unusually good weather will tend to have higher output, because bad weather hinders agricultural output. A variable like weather does not directly relate to unit inputs, so weather is considered a ____ variable.

a. Collaborative Planning, Forecasting and Replenishment
b. Total-factor productivity
c. Minimax
d. Strict liability

37. A ____ is the period of time between the initiation of any process of production and the completion of that process. Thus the ____ for ordering a new car from a manufacturer may be anywhere from 2 weeks to 6 months. In industry, ____ reduction is an important part of lean manufacturing.

a. 1990 Clean Air Act
b. 33 Strategies of War
c. 28-hour day
d. Lead time

38. ____ is a concept in economics which refers to the extent to which an enterprise or a nation actually uses its installed productive capacity. Thus, it refers to the relationship between actual output that 'is' produced with the installed equipment and the potential output which 'could' be produced with it, if capacity was fully used.

If market demand grows, ____ will rise.

a. Multifactor productivity
b. Diseconomies of scale
c. Factors of production
d. Capacity utilization

39. ____ is an inventory strategy that strives to improve the return on investment of a business by reducing in-process inventory and its associated carrying costs. To meet ____ objectives, the process relies on signals between different points in the process. This means the process is often driven by a series of signals, or Kanban, which tell production when to make the next part. Kanban are usually 'tickets' but can be simple visual signals, such as the presence or absence of a part on a shelf. Implemented correctly, ____ can dramatically improve a manufacturing organization's return on investment, quality, and efficiency.

a. 33 Strategies of War
b. 1990 Clean Air Act
c. 28-hour day
d. Just-in-time

40. ____ is, in very basic words, a position a firm occupies against its competitors.

Chapter 7. Managing Quality and Time to Create Value

According to Michael Porter, the three methods for creating a sustainable _____ are through:

1. Cost leadership

2. Differentiation

3. Focus (economics)

    a. 28-hour day
    c. Theory Z
    b. 1990 Clean Air Act
    d. Competitive advantage

41. _____ is the process whereby companies use cost accounting to report or control the various costs of doing business.

_____ generally describes the approaches and activities of managers in short run and long run planning and control decisions that increase value for customers and lower costs of products and services.

    a. Strict liability
    c. Genbutsu
    b. Missing completely at random
    d. Cost management

42. The _____ percentage shows how profitable a company's assets are in generating revenue.

_____ can be computed as:

$$\text{ROA} = \frac{\text{Net Income + Interest Expense - Interest Tax savings}}{\text{Average Total Assets}}$$

This number tells you what the company can do with what it has, i.e. how many dollars of earnings they derive from each dollar of assets they control. Its a useful number for comparing competing companies in the same industry.

    a. Return on assets
    c. Return on Capital Employed
    b. P/E ratio
    d. Return on equity

43. In business and accounting, _____s are everything of value that is owned by a person or company. Any property or object of value that one possesses, usually considered as applicable to the payment of one's debts is considered an _____. Simplistically stated, _____s are things of value that can be readily converted into cash.

    a. AAAI
    c. A Stake in the Outcome
    b. Asset
    d. A4e

Chapter 7. Managing Quality and Time to Create Value

44. In statistics, _____ is:

  • the arithmetic _____
  • the expected value of a random variable, which is also called the population _____.

It is sometimes stated that the '_____' _____s average. This is incorrect if '_____' is taken in the specific sense of 'arithmetic _____' as there are different types of averages: the _____, median, and mode. Other simple statistical analyses use measures of spread, such as range, interquartile range, or standard deviation. For a real-valued random variable X, the _____ is the expectation of X. Note that not every probability distribution has a defined _____; see the Cauchy distribution for an example.

a. Control chart
c. Mean

b. Correlation
d. Statistical inference

45. In probability theory and statistics, _____ is a measure of the variability or dispersion of a population, a data set, or a probability distribution. A low _____ indicates that the data points tend to be very close to the same value (the mean), while high _____ indicates that the data are 'spread out' over a large range of values.

For example, the average height for adult men in the United States is about 70 inches (178 cm), with a _____ of around 3 in (8 cm.)

a. Frequency distribution
c. Failure rate

b. Standard deviation
d. Normal distribution

46. _____ is a business management strategy, initially implemented by Motorola, that today enjoys widespread application in many sectors of industry.

_____ seeks to improve the quality of process outputs by identifying and removing the causes of defects (errors) and variation in manufacturing and business processes. It uses a set of quality management methods, including statistical methods, and creates a special infrastructure of people within the organization ('Black Belts' etc.)

a. Production line
c. Theory of constraints

b. Takt time
d. Six Sigma

Chapter 8. Process-Costing Systems

1. In probability theory, a probability distribution is called _____ if its cumulative distribution function is _____. This is equivalent to saying that for random variables X with the distribution in question, Pr[X = a] = 0 for all real numbers a, i.e.: the probability that X attains the value a is zero, for any number a. If the distribution of X is _____ then X is called a _____ random variable.
   a. Decision tree pruning
   b. Connectionist expert systems
   c. Pay Band
   d. Continuous

2. _____ is the production of large amounts of standardized products, including and especially on assembly lines. The concepts of _____ are applied to various kinds of products, from fluids and particulates handled in bulk to discrete solid parts to assemblies of such parts

   _____ of assemblies typically uses electric-motor-powered moving tracks or conveyor belts to move partially complete products to workers, who perform simple repetitive tasks.

   a. Mass production
   b. 1990 Clean Air Act
   c. 33 Strategies of War
   d. 28-hour day

3. _____ is an accounting methodology that traces and accumulates direct costs, and allocates indirect costs of a manufacturing process. Costs are assigned to products, usually in a large batch, which might include an entire month's production. Eventually, costs have to be allocated to individual units of product.
   a. Profit center
   b. Customer profitability
   c. Factory overhead
   d. Process costing

4. In economics, business, retail, and accounting, a _____ is the value of money that has been used up to produce something, and hence is not available for use anymore. In economics, a _____ is an alternative that is given up as a result of a decision. In business, the _____ may be one of acquisition, in which case the amount of money expended to acquire it is counted as _____.
   a. Cost overrun
   b. Cost allocation
   c. Cost
   d. Fixed costs

5. _____ is an inventory strategy that strives to improve the return on investment of a business by reducing in-process inventory and its associated carrying costs. To meet _____ objectives, the process relies on signals between different points in the process. This means the process is often driven by a series of signals, or Kanban, which tell production when to make the next part. Kanban are usually 'tickets' but can be simple visual signals, such as the presence or absence of a part on a shelf. Implemented correctly, _____ can dramatically improve a manufacturing organization's return on investment, quality, and efficiency.
   a. Just-in-time
   b. 28-hour day
   c. 33 Strategies of War
   d. 1990 Clean Air Act

6. The term _____ usually refers to a weighted arithmetic mean, but weighted versions of other means can also be calculated, such as the weighted geometric mean and the weighted harmonic mean.

Chapter 8. Process-Costing Systems

Given two school classes, one with 20 students, and one with 30 students, the grades in each class on a test were:

Morning class = 62, 67, 71, 74, 76, 77, 78, 79, 79, 80, 80, 81, 81, 82, 83, 84, 86, 89, 93, 98

Afternoon class = 81, 82, 83, 84, 85, 86, 87, 87, 88, 88, 89, 89, 89, 90, 90, 90, 90, 91, 91, 91, 92, 92, 93, 93, 94, 95, 96, 97, 98, 99

The straight average for the morning class is 80 and the straight average of the afternoon class is 90. The straight average of 80 and 90 is 85, the mean of the two class means.

a. Weighted average
b. 33 Strategies of War
c. 1990 Clean Air Act
d. 28-hour day

7. _____ is the amount of inventory a company have in stock at the end of this fiscal year. It is closely related with _____ Cost, which is the amount of money spent to get these goods in stock. It should be calculated at the Lower of Cost or Market.

a. Inventory
b. A4e
c. Ending inventory
d. A Stake in the Outcome

8. In economics, and cost accounting, _____ describes the total economic cost of production and is made up of variable costs, which vary according to the quantity of a good produced and include inputs such as labor and raw materials, plus fixed costs, which are independent of the quantity of a good produced and include inputs (capital) that cannot be varied in the short term, such as buildings and machinery. _____ in economics includes the total opportunity cost of each factor of production in addition to fixed and variable costs.

The rate at which _____ changes as the amount produced changes is called marginal cost.

a. Total cost
b. 28-hour day
c. 1990 Clean Air Act
d. 33 Strategies of War

9. A _____ is typically described as a deliberate plan of action to guide decisions and achieve rational outcome(s). However, the term may also be used to denote what is actually done, even though it is unplanned.

The term may apply to government, private sector organizations and groups, and individuals.

a. 1990 Clean Air Act
b. Policy
c. 33 Strategies of War
d. 28-hour day

10. _____ are typically small manufacturing operations that handle specialized manufacturing processes such as small customer orders or small batch jobs. _____ typically move on to different jobs (possibly with different customers) when each job is completed. By nature of this type of manufacturing operation, _____ are usually specialized in skill and processes.

a. Job shops
b. 1990 Clean Air Act
c. 33 Strategies of War
d. 28-hour day

Chapter 9. Joint-Process Costing

1. In economics, business, retail, and accounting, a _____ is the value of money that has been used up to produce something, and hence is not available for use anymore. In economics, a _____ is an alternative that is given up as a result of a decision. In business, the _____ may be one of acquisition, in which case the amount of money expended to acquire it is counted as _____.
   - a. Fixed costs
   - b. Cost allocation
   - c. Cost overrun
   - d. Cost

2. _____ is a process of attributing cost to particular cost centres. For example the wage of the driver of the purchasing department can be allocated to the purchasing department cost centre. It is not necessary to share the wage cost over several different cost centers.cost and services are not identical to each other.
   - a. Fixed costs
   - b. Cost accounting
   - c. Cost overrun
   - d. Cost allocation

3. _____ generally refers to a list of all planned expenses and revenues. It is a plan for saving and spending. A _____ is an important concept in microeconomics, which uses a _____ line to illustrate the trade-offs between two or more goods.
   - a. Budget
   - b. 1990 Clean Air Act
   - c. 28-hour day
   - d. 33 Strategies of War

4. In economics, _____ is the process by which a firm determines the price and output level that returns the greatest profit. There are several approaches to this problem. The total revenue--total cost method relies on the fact that profit equals revenue minus cost, and the marginal revenue--marginal cost method is based on the fact that total profit in a perfectly competitive market reaches its maximum point where marginal revenue equals marginal cost.
   - a. Net profit margin
   - b. Profit margin
   - c. 1990 Clean Air Act
   - d. Profit maximization

5. _____ refers to the pricing of contributions (assets, tangible and intangible, services, and funds) transferred within an organization. For example, goods from the production division may be sold to the marketing division, or goods from a parent company may be sold to a foreign subsidiary. Since the prices are set within an organization (i.e. controlled), the typical market mechanisms that establish prices for such transactions between third parties may not apply.
   - a. Transfer pricing
   - b. Price floor
   - c. Pricing
   - d. Price ceiling

6. _____ is one of the four Ps of the marketing mix. The other three aspects are product, promotion, and place. It is also a key variable in microeconomic price allocation theory.
   - a. Pricing
   - b. Price floor
   - c. Transfer pricing
   - d. Penetration pricing

7. A _____ is an entity formed between two or more parties to undertake economic activity together. The parties agree to create a new entity by both contributing equity, and they then share in the revenues, expenses, and control of the enterprise. The venture can be for one specific project only, or a continuing business relationship such as the Fuji Xerox _____.
   - a. Meritor Savings Bank v. Vinson
   - b. Patent
   - c. Civil Rights Act of 1991
   - d. Joint venture

Chapter 9. Joint-Process Costing

8. In economics, _____ is a measure of the relative satisfaction from consumption of various goods and services. Given this measure, one may speak meaningfully of increasing or decreasing _____, and thereby explain economic behavior in terms of attempts to increase one's _____. For illustrative purposes, changes in _____ are sometimes expressed in units called utils.

    a. Indirect utility function
    b. A Stake in the Outcome
    c. Ordinal utility
    d. Utility

9. An _____ is a person who has possession of an enterprise and assumes significant accountability for the inherent risks and the outcome. It is an ambitious leader who combines land, labor, and capital to create and market new goods or services. The term is a loanword from French and was first defined by the Irish economist Richard Cantillon.

    a. Entrepreneur
    b. A4e
    c. AAAI
    d. A Stake in the Outcome

10. _____ can be determined as a percentage of gross or net sales derived from use of the asset or a fixed price per unit sold. but there are also other modes and metrics of compensation. A royalty interest is the right to collect a stream of future royalty payments, often used in the oil industry and music industry to describe a percentage ownership of future production or revenues from a given leasehold, which may be divested from the original owner of the asset.

    a. Royalties
    b. National treatment
    c. Partnership agreement
    d. Railway Labor Act

Chapter 9. Joint-Process Costing

11. A _____ is a secondary or incidental product deriving from a manufacturing process, a chemical reaction or a biochemical pathway, and is not the primary product or service being produced. A _____ can be useful and marketable, or it can be considered waste.

- dried blood and blood meal - from slaughterhouse operations
- chicken _____ meal - clean parts of the carcass of slaughtered chicken, such as necks, feet, undeveloped eggs, and intestines.
- chrome shavings - from a stage of leather manufacture
- collagen and gelatin - from the boiled skin and other parts of slaughtered livestock
- feathers - from poultry processing
    - feather meal - from poultry processing
- lanolin - from the cleaning of wool
- manure - from animal husbandry
- meat and bone meal - from the rendering of animal bones and offal
- poultry byproduct and poultry meal - made from unmarketable poultry bones and offal
- poultry litter - swept from the floors of chicken coops
- whey - from cheese manufacturing
- fetal pigs

- acidulated soap stock - from the refining of vegetable oil
- bran and germ - from the milling of whole grains into refined grains
- brewer's yeast - from ethanol fermentation
- cereal food fines - from breakfast cereal processing
- corn stover - residual plant matter after harvesting of cereals
- distillers grains - from ethanol fermentation
- glycerol - from the production of biodiesel
- grape seed oil - recovered from leftovers of the winemaking process
- molasses - from sugar refining
- orange oil and other citrus oils - recovered from the peels of processed fruit
- pectin - recovered from the remains of processed fruit
- sawdust and bark- from the processing of logs into lumber
- soybean meal - from soybean processing
- straw- from grain harvesting

- asphalt - from the refining of crude oil
- fly ash - from the combustion of coal
- slag - from ore refining
- gypsum - from Flue gas desulfurization
- ash and smoke - from the combustion of fuel
- mineral oil - from refining crude oil to produce gasoline
- salt - from desalination

- sludge - from wastewater treatment

a. Jidoka
b. Homeworkers
c. Manufacturing resource planning
d. By-product

12. _____, Gross profit margin or Gross Profit Rate can be defined as the amount of contribution to the business enterprise, after paying for direct-fixed and direct-variable unit costs, required to cover overheads (fixed commitments) and provide a buffer for unknown items. It expresses the relationship between gross profit and sales revenue.

It can be expressed in absolute terms:

Gross Profit = Revenue − Cost of Sales

or as the ratio of gross profit to sales revenue, usually in the form of a percentage:

_____ Percentage = (Revenue-Cost of Sales)/Revenue

Cost of Sales includes variable costs and fixed costs directly linked to the product, such as material and labor.

a. Profit maximization
b. Gross margin
c. 1990 Clean Air Act
d. Profit margin

13. _____ is a cornerstone of accrual accounting together with the revenue recognition principle. They both determine the accounting period, in which revenues and expenses are recognized. According to the principle, expenses are recognized when obligations are (1) incurred (usually when goods are transferred or services rendered, e.g. sold), and (2) offset against recognized revenues, which were generated from those expenses (related on the cause-and-effect basis), no matter when cash is paid out.

a. Treasury stock
b. Matching principle
c. Depreciation
d. Generally accepted accounting principles

14. _____ is revenue from peripheral (non-core) operations. For example, a company that manufactures and sells automobiles would record the revenue from the sale of an automobile as 'regular' revenue. If that same company also rented a portion of one of its buildings, it would record that revenue as '_____' and disclose it separately on its income statement to show that it is from something other than its core operations.

a. Other revenue
b. Accounts receivable
c. A Stake in the Outcome
d. Accumulated Depreciation

Chapter 10. Managing and Allocating Support-Service Costs   53

1. A _____ is a special kind of database for knowledge management, providing the means for the computerized collection, organization, and retrieval of knowledge.

   _____s are categorized into two major types:

   - Machine-readable _____s store knowledge in a computer-readable form, usually for the purpose of having automated deductive reasoning applied to them. They contain a set of data, often in the form of rules that describe the knowledge in a logically consistent manner. An ontology can define the structure of stored data - what types of entities are recorded and what their relationships are. Logical operators, such as And (conjunction), Or (disjunction), material implication and negation may be used to build it up from simpler pieces of information. Consequently, classical deduction can be used to reason about the knowledge in the _____. Some machine-readable _____s are used with artificial intelligence, for example as part of an expert system that focuses on a domain like prescription drugs or customs law. Such _____s are also used by the semantic web.

   - Human-readable _____s are designed to allow people to retrieve and use the knowledge they contain. They are commonly used to complement a help desk or for sharing information among employees within an organization. They might store troubleshooting information, articles, white papers, user manuals, or answers to frequently asked questions.

   a. 1990 Clean Air Act
   c. 33 Strategies of War
   b. Knowledge base
   d. 28-hour day

2. _____ is subcontracting a process, such as product design or manufacturing, to a third-party company. The decision to outsource is often made in the interest of lowering cost or making better use of time and energy costs, redirecting or conserving energy directed at the competencies of a particular business, or to make more efficient use of land, labor, capital, (information) technology and resources. _____ became part of the business lexicon during the 1980s.
   a. Operant conditioning
   c. Unemployment insurance
   b. Opinion leadership
   d. Outsourcing

3. _____ is an advertisement in which a particular product specifically mentions a competitor by name for the express purpose of showing why the competitor is inferior to the product naming it.

This should not be confused with parody advertisements, where a fictional product is being advertised for the purpose of poking fun at the particular advertisement, nor should it be confused with the use of a coined brand name for the purpose of comparing the product without actually naming an actual competitor. ('Wikipedia tastes better and is less filling than the Encyclopedia Galactica.')

In the 1980s, during what has been referred to as the cola wars, soft-drink manufacturer Pepsi ran a series of advertisements where people, caught on hidden camera, in a blind taste test, chose Pepsi over rival Coca-Cola.

   a. 33 Strategies of War
   c. 28-hour day
   b. Comparative advertising
   d. 1990 Clean Air Act

4. In economics, business, retail, and accounting, a _____ is the value of money that has been used up to produce something, and hence is not available for use anymore. In economics, a _____ is an alternative that is given up as a result of a decision. In business, the _____ may be one of acquisition, in which case the amount of money expended to acquire it is counted as _____.
   a. Fixed costs
   b. Cost allocation
   c. Cost overrun
   d. Cost

5. _____ is information or knowledge that might result in loss of an advantage or level of security if revealed (disclosed) to others who might have low or unknown trustability and/or indeterminable or hostile intentions.

Loss, misuse, modification or unauthorized access to _____ can adversely affect the privacy of an individual, trade secrets of a business or even the security, internal and foreign affairs of a nation depending on the level of sensitivity and nature of the information.

The term classified information generally refers to information that is subject to special security classification regulations imposed by many national governments.

   a. 33 Strategies of War
   b. 1990 Clean Air Act
   c. 28-hour day
   d. Sensitive information

6. _____ refers to the pricing of contributions (assets, tangible and intangible, services, and funds) transferred within an organization. For example, goods from the production division may be sold to the marketing division, or goods from a parent company may be sold to a foreign subsidiary. Since the prices are set within an organization (i.e. controlled), the typical market mechanisms that establish prices for such transactions between third parties may not apply.
   a. Price ceiling
   b. Price floor
   c. Pricing
   d. Transfer pricing

7. _____ is one of the four Ps of the marketing mix. The other three aspects are product, promotion, and place. It is also a key variable in microeconomic price allocation theory.
   a. Penetration pricing
   b. Transfer pricing
   c. Price floor
   d. Pricing

8. _____ is a process of attributing cost to particular cost centres. For example the wage of the driver of the purchasing department can be allocated to the purchasing department cost centre. It is not necessary to share the wage cost over several different cost centers.cost and services are not identical to each other.
   a. Cost accounting
   b. Cost overrun
   c. Fixed costs
   d. Cost allocation

9. _____ can be regarded as an outcome of mental processes (cognitive process) leading to the selection of a course of action among several alternatives. Every _____ process produces a final choice. The output can be an action or an opinion of choice.
   a. 33 Strategies of War
   b. 28-hour day
   c. Decision making
   d. 1990 Clean Air Act

10. _____ is a technical term used in management science popularized by Joseph M. Juran

Chapter 10. Managing and Allocating Support-Service Costs

He defined an internal and external customers as anyone affected by the product or by the process used to produce the product, in the context of quality management. _____s may play the role as supplier, processer, and customer in the sequence of product development.

He claimed that the organization must understand and identify both internal and external customers and their needs.

a. AAAI
b. A4e
c. A Stake in the Outcome
d. Internal customer

11. _____ is a costing model that identifies activities in an organization and assigns the cost of each activity resource to all products and services according to the actual consumption by each: it assigns more indirect costs (overhead) into direct costs.

In this way an organization can establish the true cost of its individual products and services for the purposes of identifying and eliminating those which are unprofitable and lowering the prices of those which are overpriced.

In a business organization, the ABC methodology assigns an organization's resource costs through activities to the products and services provided to its customers.

a. Indirect costs
b. Activity-based costing
c. A4e
d. A Stake in the Outcome

12. _____ is an increasingly broadening term with which an organization, or other human system describes the combination of traditionally administrative personnel functions with acquisition and application of skills, knowledge and experience, Employee Relations and resource planning at various levels. The field draws upon concepts developed in Industrial/Organizational Psychology and System Theory. _____ has at least two related interpretations depending on context. The original usage derives from political economy and economics, where it was traditionally called labor, one of four factors of production although this perspective is changing as a function of new and ongoing research into more strategic approaches at national levels. This first usage is used more in terms of '_____ development', and can go beyond just organizations to the level of nations . The more traditional usage within corporations and businesses refers to the individuals within a firm or agency, and to the portion of the organization that deals with hiring, firing, training, and other personnel issues, typically referred to as `_____ management'.

a. Human resource management
b. Bradford Factor
c. Progressive discipline
d. Human Resources

13. In the fields of science, engineering, industry and statistics, _____ is the degree of closeness of a measured or calculated quantity to its actual (true) value. _____ is closely related to precision, also called reproducibility or repeatability, the degree to which further measurements or calculations show the same or similar results. _____ indicates proximity to the true value, precision to the repeatability or reproducibility of the measurement

The results of calculations or a measurement can be accurate but not precise, precise but not accurate, neither, or both.

a. AAAI
b. A Stake in the Outcome
c. Accuracy
d. A4e

14. _____ is one of the four elements of marketing mix. An organization or set of organizations (go-betweens) involved in the process of making a product or service available for use or consumption by a consumer or business user.

The other three parts of the marketing mix are product, pricing, and promotion.

a. Job creation programs
b. Distribution
c. Missing completely at random
d. Matching theory

15. A _____ is a type of business entity in which partners (owners) share with each other the profits or losses of the business. _____s are often favored over corporations for taxation purposes, as the _____ structure does not generally incur a tax on profits before it is distributed to the partners (i.e. there is no dividend tax levied.) However, depending on the _____ structure and the jurisdiction in which it operates, owners of a _____ may be exposed to greater personal liability than they would as shareholders of a corporation.

a. Mediation
b. Due process
c. Partnership
d. Federal Employers Liability Act

Chapter 11. Cost Estimation

1. In economics, business, retail, and accounting, a _____ is the value of money that has been used up to produce something, and hence is not available for use anymore. In economics, a _____ is an alternative that is given up as a result of a decision. In business, the _____ may be one of acquisition, in which case the amount of money expended to acquire it is counted as _____.
   a. Fixed costs
   b. Cost overrun
   c. Cost allocation
   d. Cost

2. _____ is an area of engineering practice concerned with the 'application of scientific principles and techniques to problems of cost estimating, cost control, business planning and management science, profitability analysis, project management, and planning and scheduling.'

   Key objectives of _____ are to arrive at accurate cost estimates and to avoid cost overruns. The broad array of _____ topics represent the intersection of the fields of project management, business management, and engineering. Most people have a limited view of what engineering encompasses.

   a. 1990 Clean Air Act
   b. 28-hour day
   c. 33 Strategies of War
   d. Cost engineering

3. _____ is the process whereby companies use cost accounting to report or control the various costs of doing business.

   _____ generally describes the approaches and activities of managers in short run and long run planning and control decisions that increase value for customers and lower costs of products and services.

   a. Genbutsu
   b. Cost management
   c. Missing completely at random
   d. Strict liability

4. _____ can be regarded as an outcome of mental processes (cognitive process) leading to the selection of a course of action among several alternatives. Every _____ process produces a final choice. The output can be an action or an opinion of choice.
   a. 33 Strategies of War
   b. 28-hour day
   c. 1990 Clean Air Act
   d. Decision making

5. _____ is a process of attributing cost to particular cost centres. For example the wage of the driver of the purchasing department can be allocated to the purchasing department cost centre. It is not necessary to share the wage cost over several different cost centers.cost and services are not identical to each other.
   a. Cost accounting
   b. Fixed costs
   c. Cost overrun
   d. Cost allocation

6. _____ is an organization's process of defining its strategy and making decisions on allocating its resources to pursue this strategy, including its capital and people. Various business analysis techniques can be used in _____, including SWOT analysis (Strengths, Weaknesses, Opportunities, and Threats) and PEST analysis (Political, Economic, Social, and Technological analysis) or STEER analysis involving Socio-cultural, Technological, Economic, Ecological, and Regulatory factors and EPISTEL (Environment, Political, Informatic, Social, Technological, Economic and Legal)

Chapter 11. Cost Estimation

_____ is the formal consideration of an organization's future course. All _____ deals with at least one of three key questions:

1. 'What do we do?'
2. 'For whom do we do it?'
3. 'How do we excel?'

In business _____, the third question is better phrased 'How can we beat or avoid competition?'. (Bradford and Duncan, page 1.)

a. 33 Strategies of War
b. 28-hour day
c. 1990 Clean Air Act
d. Strategic planning

7. _____s are expenses that change in proportion to the activity of a business. In other words, _____ is the sum of marginal costs. It can also be considered normal costs.

a. Cost accounting
b. Fixed costs
c. Cost overrun
d. Variable cost

8. _____ are formal records of the financial activities of a business, person, or other entity. In British English, including United Kingdom company law, _____ are often referred to as accounts, although the term _____ is also used, particularly by accountants.

_____ provide an overview of a business or person's financial condition in both short and long term.

a. 28-hour day
b. Financial statements
c. 33 Strategies of War
d. 1990 Clean Air Act

9. The terms '_____' and 'independent variable' are used in similar but subtly different ways in mathematics and statistics as part of the standard terminology in those subjects. They are used to distinguish between two types of quantities being considered, separating them into those available at the start of a process and those being created by it, where the latter (_____s) are dependent on the former (independent variables.)

The independent variable is typically the variable being manipulated or changed and the _____ is the observed result of the independent variable being manipulated.

a. 28-hour day
b. Taguchi methods
c. 1990 Clean Air Act
d. Dependent variable

10. In statistics, _____ refers to techniques for the modeling and analysis of numerical data consisting of values of a dependent variable and of one or more independent variables The dependent variable in the regression equation is modeled as a function of the independent variables, corresponding parameters, and an error term. The error term is treated as a random variable and represents unexplained variation in the dependent variable.

a. Least squares
b. Stepwise regression
c. Trend analysis
d. Regression analysis

Chapter 11. Cost Estimation

11. In statistics, an _____ is an observation that is numerically distant from the rest of the data.

They can occur by chance in any distribution, but they are often indicative either of measurement error or that the population has a heavy-tailed distribution. In the former case one wishes to discard them or use statistics that are robust to _____s, while in the latter case they indicate that the distribution has high kurtosis and that one should be very cautious in using tool or intuitions that assume a normal distribution.

a. AAAI
b. A Stake in the Outcome
c. Outlier
d. A4e

12. In business, overhead, _____ or overhead expense refers to an ongoing expense of operating a business. The term overhead is usually used to group expenses that are necessary to the continued functioning of the business, but do not directly generate profits.

Overhead expenses are all costs on the income statement except for direct labor and direct materials.

a. Intangible assets
b. Interlocking directorate
c. Industrial market segmentation
d. Overhead cost

13. In economics, _____ is a rise in the general level of prices of goods and services in an economy over a period of time. When the general price level rises, each unit of the functional currency buys fewer goods and services; consequently, _____ is a decline in the real value of money--a loss of purchasing power in the internal medium of exchange which is also the monetary unit of account in an economy. A chief measure of general price-level _____ is the general _____ rate, which is the percentage change in a general price index (normally the Consumer Price Index) over time.

a. A Stake in the Outcome
b. A4e
c. Economy
d. Inflation

14. In statistics, _____ are a common occurrence. Several statistical methods have been developed to deal with this problem. _____ mean that no data value is stored for the variable in the current observation.

a. 28-hour day
b. 33 Strategies of War
c. Missing values
d. 1990 Clean Air Act

15. The _____ of a product is the cost per standard unit supplied, which may be a single sample or a container of a given number. When purchasing more than a single unit, the total cost will increase with the number of units, but it is common for the _____ to decrease as quantity is increased (bulk purchasing), as there are discounts etc. This reduction in long run _____s which arise from an increase in production/purchasing is due to the fixed costs being spread out over more products and is called economies of scale.

a. A4e
b. A Stake in the Outcome
c. Unit cost
d. AAAI

16. The _____ of a statistical model describes how well it fits a set of observations. Measures of _____ typically summarize the discrepancy between observed values and the values expected under the model in question. Such measures can be used in statistical hypothesis testing, e.g. to test for normality of residuals, to test whether two samples are drawn from identical distributions , or whether outcome frequencies follow a specified distribution

a. Law of the iterated logarithm
b. Pareto Analysis
c. Location-scale family
d. Goodness of fit

17. In statistics, a result is called _____ if it is unlikely to have occurred by chance. 'A _____ difference' simply means there is statistical evidence that there is a difference; it does not mean the difference is necessarily large, important, or significant in the common meaning of the word.

The significance level of a test is a traditional frequentist statistical hypothesis testing concept.

a. Generalized normal distribution
b. Simple moving average
c. Statistics
d. Statistically significant

18. _____ consists of the mental process of thinking involved with the process of judging the merits of multiple options and selecting one of them for action. Some simple examples include deciding whether to get up in the morning or go back to sleep, or selecting a given route for a journey. More complex examples (often decisions that affect what a person thinks or their core beliefs) include choosing a lifestyle, religious affiliation, or political position.

a. Groups decision making
b. Trade study
c. Championship mobilization
d. Choice

19. _____ is the process of estimation in unknown situations. Prediction is a similar, but more general term. Both can refer to estimation of time series, cross-sectional or longitudinal data.

a. 33 Strategies of War
b. 1990 Clean Air Act
c. 28-hour day
d. Forecasting

20. _____ is subcontracting a process, such as product design or manufacturing, to a third-party company. The decision to outsource is often made in the interest of lowering cost or making better use of time and energy costs, redirecting or conserving energy directed at the competencies of a particular business, or to make more efficient use of land, labor, capital, (information) technology and resources. _____ became part of the business lexicon during the 1980s.

a. Opinion leadership
b. Operant conditioning
c. Unemployment insurance
d. Outsourcing

21. _____ is a strategic planning method that some organizations use to make flexible long-term plans. It is in large part an adaptation and generalization of classic methods used by military intelligence.

The original method was that a group of analysts would generate simulation games for policy makers. In business applications, the emphasis on gaming the behavior of opponents was reduced (shifting more toward a game against nature). At Royal Dutch/Shell for example, _____ was viewed as changing mindsets about the exogenous part of the world, prior to formulating specific strategies.

a. Time and attendance
b. Retroactive overtime
c. Labour productivity
d. Scenario planning

22. _____ is the study of how the variation (uncertainty) in the output of a mathematical model can be apportioned, qualitatively or quantitatively, to different sources of variation in the input of a model.

In more general terms uncertainty and sensitivity analyses investigate the robustness of a study when the study includes some form of mathematical modelling. While uncertainty analysis studies the overall uncertainty in the conclusions of the study, _____ tries to identify what source of uncertainty weights more on the study's conclusions.

    a. Policies and procedures
    c. No-bid contract
    b. Foreign ownership
    d. Sensitivity analysis

23. The method of _____ is used to approximately solve overdetermined systems, i.e. systems of equations in which there are more equations than unknowns. _____ is often applied in statistical contexts, particularly regression analysis.

_____ can be interpreted as a method of fitting data.

    a. Regression analysis
    c. Trend analysis
    b. Least squares
    d. Stepwise regression

24. In statistics, a _____ is, broadly speaking, a statistic whose sampling distribution is a Student's t-distribution. These are a parametric statistic, most frequently used in statistical hypothesis testing in Student's t-tests, but can be defined and used independently of hypothesis testing.

Broadly speaking, a _____ is any statistic whose sampling distribution is a Student's t-distribution.

    a. T-statistic
    c. 1990 Clean Air Act
    b. Skewness risk
    d. Kurtosis risk

25. _____ is the cross-correlation of a signal with itself. It is a mathematical tool for finding repeating patterns, such as the presence of a periodic signal which has been buried under noise, or identifying the missing fundamental frequency in a signal implied by its harmonic frequencies. It is used frequently in signal processing for analyzing functions or series of values, such as time domain signals.
    a. AAAI
    c. A Stake in the Outcome
    b. A4e
    d. Autocorrelation

26. In statistics, a sequence of random variables is _____ if the random variables have different variances. The term means 'differing variance' and comes from the Greek 'hetero' and 'skedasis' ('dispersion'.) In contrast, a sequence of random variables is called homoskedastic if it has constant variance.
    a. Standard deviation
    c. Heteroskedastic
    b. Random variables
    d. Probability

27. In statistics, a sequence or a vector of random variables is _____ if all random variables in the sequence or vector have the same finite variance. This is also known as homogeneity of variance. The complementary notion is called heteroskedasticity.
    a. Time series
    c. Location parameter
    b. Standard deviation
    d. Homoscedastic

28. In statistics, _____ indicates the strength and direction of a linear relationship between two random variables. That is in contrast with the usage of the term in colloquial speech, which denotes any relationship, not necessarily linear. In general statistical usage, _____ or co-relation refers to the departure of two random variables from independence.
   a. Median
   b. Time series analysis
   c. Correlation
   d. Heteroskedastic

29. The term _____ refers to a graphical representation of the 'average' rate of learning for an activity or tool. It can represent at a glance the initial difficulty of learning something and, to an extent, how much there is to learn after initial familiarity. For example, the Windows program Notepad is extremely simple to learn, but offers little after this.
   a. 33 Strategies of War
   b. 28-hour day
   c. 1990 Clean Air Act
   d. Learning curve

30. _____ is an area of knowledge within organizational theory that studies models and theories about the way an organization learns and adapts.

In Organizational development (OD), learning is a characteristic of an adaptive organization, i.e., an organization that is able to sense changes in signals from its environment (both internal and external) and adapt accordingly.

   a. A Stake in the Outcome
   b. AAAI
   c. Organizational learning
   d. A4e

31. _____ is, in very basic words, a position a firm occupies against its competitors.

According to Michael Porter, the three methods for creating a sustainable _____ are through:

1. Cost leadership

2. Differentiation

3. Focus (economics)

   a. Theory Z
   b. 28-hour day
   c. 1990 Clean Air Act
   d. Competitive advantage

Chapter 12. Financial and CostVolume-Profit Models

1. _____ is the task of building an abstract representation (a model) of a financial decision making situation. This is a mathematical model, such as a computer simulation, designed to represent (a simplified version of) the performance of a financial asset or a portfolio, of a business, a project, or any other form of financial investment.

_____ is a general term that means different things to different users.

   a. Risk
   b. Financial modeling
   c. Panjer recursion
   d. Discounting

2. _____s are statistical models used in econometrics. An _____ specifies the statistical relationship that is believed to hold between the various economic quantities pertaining a particular economic phenomena under study. An _____ can be derived from a deterministic economic model by allowing for uncertainty or from an economic model which itself is stochastic.

   a. Econometric model
   b. AAAI
   c. A Stake in the Outcome
   d. A4e

3. _____ is a company's financial statement that indicates how the revenue is transformed into the net income The purpose of the _____ is to show managers and investors whether the company made or lost money during the period being reported.

The important thing to remember about an _____ is that it represents a period of time.

   a. A4e
   b. Income statement
   c. A Stake in the Outcome
   d. AAAI

4. _____ are formal records of the financial activities of a business, person, or other entity. In British English, including United Kingdom company law, _____ are often referred to as accounts, although the term _____ is also used, particularly by accountants.

_____ provide an overview of a business or person's financial condition in both short and long term.

   a. 28-hour day
   b. 1990 Clean Air Act
   c. 33 Strategies of War
   d. Financial statements

5. _____ of the learning curve effect and the closely related experience curve effect express the relationship between equations for experience and efficiency or between efficiency gains and investment in the effort. The experience of 'learning curves' was first observed by the 19th Century German psychologist Hermann Ebbinghaus according to the difficulty of memorizing varying numbers of verbal stimuli, and subsequent learning about the complex processes of learning are discussed in the

.

The rule used for representing the learning curve effect states that the more times a task has been performed, the less time will be required on each subsequent iteration.

Chapter 12. Financial and CostVolume-Profit Models

    a. Models
    b. Point biserial correlation coefficient
    c. Spatial Decision Support Systems
    d. Distribution

6. _____ can be regarded as an outcome of mental processes (cognitive process) leading to the selection of a course of action among several alternatives. Every _____ process produces a final choice. The output can be an action or an opinion of choice.
    a. 1990 Clean Air Act
    b. 33 Strategies of War
    c. 28-hour day
    d. Decision making

7. In economics, business, retail, and accounting, a _____ is the value of money that has been used up to produce something, and hence is not available for use anymore. In economics, a _____ is an alternative that is given up as a result of a decision. In business, the _____ may be one of acquisition, in which case the amount of money expended to acquire it is counted as _____.
    a. Cost overrun
    b. Fixed costs
    c. Cost allocation
    d. Cost

8. _____ is a process of attributing cost to particular cost centres. For example the wage of the driver of the purchasing department can be allocated to the purchasing department cost centre. It is not necessary to share the wage cost over several different cost centers.cost and services are not identical to each other.
    a. Fixed costs
    b. Cost accounting
    c. Cost overrun
    d. Cost allocation

9. In economics ' business, specifically cost accounting, the _____ is the point at which cost or expenses and revenue are equal: there is no net loss or gain, and one has 'broken even'. A profit or a loss has not been made, although opportunity costs have been paid, and capital has received the risk-adjusted, expected return.

For example, if the business sells less than 200 tables each month, it will make a loss, if it sells more, it will be a profit.

    a. Fixed asset turnover
    b. Defined benefit pension plan
    c. Virtuous circle
    d. Break-even point

10. In cost-volume-profit analysis, a form of management accounting, _____ is the marginal profit per unit sale. It is a useful quantity in carrying out various calculations, and can be used as a measure of operating leverage.

The Total _____ is Total Revenue (TR, or Sales) minus Total Variable Cost (TVC):

    TContribution margin = TR − TVC

The Unit _____ (C) is Unit Revenue (Price, P) minus Unit Variable Cost (V):

    C = P − V

The _____ Ratio is the percentage of Contribution over Total Revenue, which can be calculated from the unit contribution over unit price or total contribution over Total Revenue:

$$\frac{C}{P} = \frac{P - V}{P} = \frac{\text{Unit Contribution Margin}}{\text{Price}} = \frac{\text{Total Contribution Margin}}{\text{Total Revenue}}$$

For instance, if the price is $10 and the unit variable cost is $2, then the unit _____ is $8, and the _____ ratio is $8/$10 = 80%.

a. Factory overhead
c. Profit center
b. Customer profitability
d. Contribution margin

11. In economics, _____ are business expenses that are not dependent on the activities of the business They tend to be time-related, such as salaries or rents being paid per month. This is in contrast to variable costs, which are volume-related (and are paid per quantity.)

In management accounting, _____ are defined as expenses that do not change in proportion to the activity of a business, within the relevant period or scale of production.

a. Transaction cost
c. Cost of quality
b. Cost allocation
d. Fixed costs

12. The _____ is a measure of how revenue growth translates into growth in operating income. It is a measure of leverage, and of how risky (volatile) a company's operating income is.

There are various measures of _____, which can be interpreted analogously to financial leverage.

a. A Stake in the Outcome
c. AAAI
b. Operating leverage
d. A4e

13. 'Speaking generally, properties are those physical quantities which directly describe the physical attributes of the system; _____s are those combinations of the properties which suffice to determine the response of the system. Properties can have all sorts of dimensions, depending upon the system being considered; _____s are dimensionless, or have the dimension of time or its reciprocal.'

The term can also be used in engineering contexts, however, as it is typically used in the physical sciences.

When the terms formal _____ and actual _____ are used, they generally correspond with the definitions used in computer science.

a. 1990 Clean Air Act
c. 33 Strategies of War
b. 28-hour day
d. Parameter

Chapter 12. Financial and CostVolume-Profit Models

14. _____ is a costing model that identifies activities in an organization and assigns the cost of each activity resource to all products and services according to the actual consumption by each: it assigns more indirect costs (overhead) into direct costs.

In this way an organization can establish the true cost of its individual products and services for the purposes of identifying and eliminating those which are unprofitable and lowering the prices of those which are overpriced.

In a business organization, the ABC methodology assigns an organization's resource costs through activities to the products and services provided to its customers.

    a. A Stake in the Outcome   b. Activity-based costing
    c. A4e   d. Indirect costs

15. _____ is a strategic planning method that some organizations use to make flexible long-term plans. It is in large part an adaptation and generalization of classic methods used by military intelligence.

The original method was that a group of analysts would generate simulation games for policy makers. In business applications, the emphasis on gaming the behavior of opponents was reduced (shifting more toward a game against nature). At Royal Dutch/Shell for example, _____ was viewed as changing mindsets about the exogenous part of the world, prior to formulating specific strategies.

    a. Retroactive overtime   b. Time and attendance
    c. Labour productivity   d. Scenario planning

16. _____ is the study of how the variation (uncertainty) in the output of a mathematical model can be apportioned, qualitatively or quantitatively, to different sources of variation in the input of a model .

In more general terms uncertainty and sensitivity analyses investigate the robustness of a study when the study includes some form of mathematical modelling. While uncertainty analysis studies the overall uncertainty in the conclusions of the study, _____ tries to identify what source of uncertainty weights more on the study's conclusions.

    a. No-bid contract   b. Policies and procedures
    c. Foreign ownership   d. Sensitivity analysis

17. _____ is an overall management philosophy introduced by Dr. Eliyahu M. Goldratt in his 1984 book titled The Goal, that is geared to help organizations continually achieve their goal. The title comes from the contention that any manageable system is limited in achieving more of its goal by a very small number of constraints, and that there is always at least one constraint. The _____ process seeks to identify the constraint and restructure the rest of the organization around it, through the use of the Five Focusing Steps.
    a. Six Sigma   b. Takt time
    c. Production line   d. Theory of Constraints

18. In optimization (a branch of mathematics), a _____ is a member of a set of possible solutions to a given problem. A _____ does not have to be a likely or reasonable solution to the problem. The space of all _____ s is called the feasible region, feasible set, search space, or solution space.

a. 1990 Clean Air Act
b. Hann function
c. Gibbs state
d. Candidate solution

19. In mathematics, _____ is a technique for optimization of a linear objective function, subject to linear equality and linear inequality constraints. Informally, _____ determines the way to achieve the best outcome (such as maximum profit or lowest cost) in a given mathematical model and given some list of requirements represented as linear equations.

More formally, given a polytope (for example, a polygon or a polyhedron), and a real-valued affine function

$$f(x_1, x_2, \ldots, x_n) = c_1 x_1 + c_2 x_2 + \cdots + c_n x_n + d$$

defined on this polytope, a _____ method will find a point in the polytope where this function has the smallest (or largest) value.

a. Linear programming relaxation
b. 1990 Clean Air Act
c. Slack variable
d. Linear programming

20. The function f is called, variously, an _____, cost function, energy function, or energy functional. A feasible solution that minimizes (or maximizes, if that is the goal) the _____ is called an optimal solution.

Generally, when the feasible region or the _____ of the problem does not present convexity, there may be several local minima and maxima, where a local minimum x^* is defined as a point for which there exists some $>\delta > 0$ so that for all x such that

the expression

holds; that is to say, on some region around x^* all of the function values are greater than or equal to the value at that point.

a. Objective function
b. AAAI
c. A Stake in the Outcome
d. A4e

Chapter 13. Cost Management and Decision Making

1. A _____ is the term given to a company that facilitates the learning of its members and continuously transforms itself. _____s develop as a result of the pressures facing modern organizations and enables them to remain competitive in the business environment. A _____ has five main features; systems thinking, personal mastery, mental models, shared vision and team learning.
   a. 1990 Clean Air Act
   b. Learning organization
   c. Quality function deployment
   d. Hoshin Kanri

2. In the fields of science, engineering, industry and statistics, _____ is the degree of closeness of a measured or calculated quantity to its actual (true) value. _____ is closely related to precision, also called reproducibility or repeatability, the degree to which further measurements or calculations show the same or similar results. _____ indicates proximity to the true value, precision to the repeatability or reproducibility of the measurement

   The results of calculations or a measurement can be accurate but not precise, precise but not accurate, neither, or both.

   a. A4e
   b. AAAI
   c. Accuracy
   d. A Stake in the Outcome

3. In economics, business, retail, and accounting, a _____ is the value of money that has been used up to produce something, and hence is not available for use anymore. In economics, a _____ is an alternative that is given up as a result of a decision. In business, the _____ may be one of acquisition, in which case the amount of money expended to acquire it is counted as _____.
   a. Fixed costs
   b. Cost
   c. Cost overrun
   d. Cost allocation

4. _____ is the difference between the revenues earned from and the costs associated with the customer relationship in a specified period.

   According to Philip Kotler,'a profitable customer is a person, household or a company that overtime, yields a revenue stream that exceeds by an acceptable amount the company's cost stream of attracting, selling and servicing the customer'

   Although _____ is nothing more than the result of applying the business concept of profit to a customer relationship, measuring the profitability of a firm's customers or customer groups can often deliver useful business insights.

   Quite often a very small percentage of the firm's best customers will account for a large portion of firm profit.

   a. Customer profitability
   b. Factory overhead
   c. Profit center
   d. Process costing

5. A _____ is the belief that there is a technique, method, process, activity, incentive or reward that is more effective at delivering a particular outcome than any other technique, method, process, etc. The idea is that with proper processes, checks, and testing, a desired outcome can be delivered with fewer problems and unforeseen complications. _____s can also be defined as the most efficient (least amount of effort) and effective (best results) way of accomplishing a task, based on repeatable procedures that have proven themselves over time for large numbers of people.

a. Design management
b. Fix it twice
c. Hierarchical organization
d. Best practice

6. _____ is a phrase that describes a situation where the opportunity cost of decision analysis exceeds the benefits that could be gained by enacting some decision thus preventing a decision. The phrase applies to any situation where analysis may be applied to help make a decision and may be a dysfunctional element of organizational behavior. This is often phrased as paralysis by analysis, in contrast to extinct by instinct.
   a. A Stake in the Outcome
   b. Analysis paralysis
   c. A4e
   d. AAAI

7. A _____ is a professional who provides advice in a particular area of expertise such as management, accountancy, the environment, entertainment, technology, law, human resources, marketing, medicine, finance, economics, public affairs, communication, engineering, sound system design, graphic design, or waste management.

A _____ is usually an expert or a professional in a specific field and has a wide knowledge of the subject matter. A _____ usually works for a consultancy firm or is self-employed, and engages with multiple and changing clients.

   a. 1990 Clean Air Act
   b. 33 Strategies of War
   c. Consultant
   d. 28-hour day

8. A _____ is a decision support tool that uses a tree-like graph or model of decisions and their possible consequences, including chance event outcomes, resource costs, and utility. _____s are commonly used in operations research, specifically in decision analysis, to help identify a strategy most likely to reach a goal. Another use of _____s is as a descriptive means for calculating conditional probabilities.
   a. Decision tree
   b. 1990 Clean Air Act
   c. 33 Strategies of War
   d. 28-hour day

9. In game theory, an _____ is a set of moves or strategies taken by the players, or their payoffs resulting from the actions or strategies taken by all players. The two are complementary in that given knowledge of the set of strategies of all players, the final state of the game is known, as are any relevant payoffs. In a game where chance or a random event is involved, the _____ is not known from only the set of strategies, but is only realized when the random event(s) are realized.
   a. AAAI
   b. A4e
   c. A Stake in the Outcome
   d. Outcome

10. In economics and business decision-making, _____ are costs that cannot be recovered once they have been incurred. _____ are sometimes contrasted with variable costs, which are the costs that will change due to the proposed course of action, and prospective costs which are costs that will be incurred if an action is taken.

In traditional microeconomic theory, only variable costs are relevant to a decision.

   a. Fundamental attribution error
   b. Pygmalion effect
   c. Cognitive biases
   d. Sunk costs

11. _____ is subcontracting a process, such as product design or manufacturing, to a third-party company. The decision to outsource is often made in the interest of lowering cost or making better use of time and energy costs, redirecting or conserving energy directed at the competencies of a particular business, or to make more efficient use of land, labor, capital, (information) technology and resources. _____ became part of the business lexicon during the 1980s.

   a. Outsourcing   b. Opinion leadership
   c. Operant conditioning   d. Unemployment insurance

12. The _____ is a concept from business management that was first described and popularized by Michael Porter in his 1985 best-seller, Competitive Advantage: Creating and Sustaining Superior Performance.

A _____ is a chain of activities. Products pass through all activities of the chain in order and at each activity the product gains some value. The chain of activities gives the products more added value than the sum of added values of all activities. It is important not to mix the concept of the _____ with the costs occurring throughout the activities.

   a. Customer relationship management   b. Mass marketing
   c. Market development   d. Value chain

13. A _____ is a type of business entity in which partners (owners) share with each other the profits or losses of the business. _____s are often favored over corporations for taxation purposes, as the _____ structure does not generally incur a tax on profits before it is distributed to the partners (i.e. there is no dividend tax levied.) However, depending on the _____ structure and the jurisdiction in which it operates, owners of a _____ may be exposed to greater personal liability than they would as shareholders of a corporation.

   a. Due process   b. Federal Employers Liability Act
   c. Partnership   d. Mediation

14. _____ is an advertisement in which a particular product specifically mentions a competitor by name for the express purpose of showing why the competitor is inferior to the product naming it.

This should not be confused with parody advertisements, where a fictional product is being advertised for the purpose of poking fun at the particular advertisement, nor should it be confused with the use of a coined brand name for the purpose of comparing the product without actually naming an actual competitor. ('Wikipedia tastes better and is less filling than the Encyclopedia Galactica.')

In the 1980s, during what has been referred to as the cola wars, soft-drink manufacturer Pepsi ran a series of advertisements where people, caught on hidden camera, in a blind taste test, chose Pepsi over rival Coca-Cola.

   a. 28-hour day   b. Comparative advertising
   c. 33 Strategies of War   d. 1990 Clean Air Act

15. _____ is one of the four Ps of the marketing mix. The other three aspects are product, promotion, and place. It is also a key variable in microeconomic price allocation theory.

   a. Transfer pricing   b. Penetration pricing
   c. Price floor   d. Pricing

Chapter 13. Cost Management and Decision Making

16. _____ was a writer, management consultant, and self-described 'social ecologist.' Widely considered to be 'the father of modern management,' his 39 books and countless scholarly and popular articles explored how humans are organized across all sectors of society--in business, government and the nonprofit world. His writings have predicted many of the major developments of the late twentieth century, including privatization and decentralization; the rise of Japan to economic world power; the decisive importance of marketing; and the emergence of the information society with its necessity of lifelong learning. In 1959, Drucker coined the term 'knowledge worker' and later in his life considered knowledge work productivity to be the next frontier of management.

   a. Debora L. Spar
   b. Chrissie Hynde
   c. Jacques Al-Salawat Nasruddin Nasser
   d. Peter Ferdinand Drucker

17. _____ is the difference between the cost of a good or service and its selling price. A _____ is added on to the total cost incurred by the producer of a good or service in order to create a profit. The total cost reflects the total amount of both fixed and variable expenses to produce and distribute a product.

   a. Topics
   b. Premium pricing
   c. Price points
   d. Markup

18. _____ Management is the succession of strategies used by management as a product goes through its _____. The conditions in which a product is sold changes over time and must be managed as it moves through its succession of stages.

   The _____ goes through many phases, involves many professional disciplines, and requires many skills, tools and processes.

   a. Product life cycle
   b. Strategic Alliance
   c. Job hunting
   d. Golden handshake

19. _____, known in the United States as antitrust law, has three main elements:

   - prohibiting agreements or practices that restrict free trading and competition between business entities. This includes in particular the repression of cartels.
   - banning abusive behavior by a firm dominating a market, or anti-competitive practices that tend to lead to such a dominant position. Practices controlled in this way may include predatory pricing, tying, price gouging, refusal to deal, and many others.
   - supervising the mergers and acquisitions of large corporations, including some joint ventures. Transactions that are considered to threaten the competitive process can be prohibited altogether, or approved subject to 'remedies' such as an obligation to divest part of the merged business or to offer licenses or access to facilities to enable other businesses to continue competing.

   The substance and practice of _____ varies from jurisdiction to jurisdiction. Protecting the interests of consumers (consumer welfare) and ensuring that entrepreneurs have an opportunity to compete in the market economy are often treated as important objectives. _____ is closely connected with law on deregulation of access to markets, state aids and subsidies, the privatization of state owned assets and the establishment of independent sector regulators. In recent decades, _____ has been viewed as a way to provide better public services.

a. Federal Employers Liability Act
b. Rulemaking
c. Right to Financial Privacy Act
d. Competition law

20. _____ exists when sales of identical goods or services are transacted at different prices from the same provider. In a theoretical market with perfect information, no transaction costs or prohibition on secondary exchange (or re-selling) to prevent arbitrage, _____ can only be a feature of monopoly and oligopoly markets, where market power can be exercised. Otherwise, the moment the seller tries to sell the same good at different prices, the buyer at the lower price can arbitrage by selling to the consumer buying at the higher price but with a tiny discount.
   a. Price points
   b. Pricing objectives
   c. Target costing
   d. Price discrimination

21. The _____ of 1936 (or Anti-Price Discrimination Act, 15 U.S.C. §13) is a United States federal law that prohibits what were considered, at the time of passage, to be anticompetitive practices by producers, specifically price discrimination. It grew out of practices in which chain stores were allowed to purchase goods at lower prices than other retailers.
   a. Bona fide occupational qualification
   b. Privity
   c. Robinson-Patman Act
   d. Labor Management Reporting and Disclosure Act

22. _____ is the practice of selling a product or service at a very low price, intending to drive competitors out of the market, or create barriers to entry for potential new competitors. If competitors or potential competitors cannot sustain equal or lower prices without losing money, they go out of business or choose not to enter the business. The predatory merchant then has fewer competitors or is even a de facto monopoly, and can then raise prices above what the market would otherwise bear.
   a. Predatory pricing
   b. Collusion
   c. 28-hour day
   d. 1990 Clean Air Act

Chapter 14. Strategic Issues in Making Investment Decisions

1. _____ is the planning process used to determine whether a firm's long term investments such as new machinery, replacement machinery, new plants, new products, and research development projects are worth pursuing. It is budget for major capital, or investment, expenditures.

Many formal methods are used in _____, including the techniques such as

- Net present value
- Profitability index
- Internal rate of return
- Modified Internal Rate of Return
- Equivalent annuity

These methods use the incremental cash flows from each potential investment, or project. Techniques based on accounting earnings and accounting rules are sometimes used - though economists consider this to be improper - such as the accounting rate of return, and 'return on investment.' Simplified and hybrid methods are used as well, such as payback period and discounted payback period.

a. Restricted stock
c. Gross profit margin
b. Capital budgeting
d. Gross profit

2. In finance, the _____ approach describes a method of valuing a project, company, or asset using the concepts of the time value of money. All future cash flows are estimated and discounted to give their present values. The discount rate used is generally the appropriate WACC, that reflects the risk of the cashflows.
a. 1990 Clean Air Act
c. Present value
b. Net present value
d. Discounted cash flow

3. _____ or net present worth (NPW) is defined as the total present value (PV) of a time series of cash flows. It is a standard method for using the time value of money to appraise long-term projects. Used for capital budgeting, and widely throughout economics, it measures the excess or shortfall of cash flows, in present value terms, once financing charges are met.
a. Net present value
c. 1990 Clean Air Act
b. Present value
d. Discounted cash flow

4. _____ refers to the movement of cash into or out of a business or financial product. It is usually measured during a specified, finite period of time. Measurement of _____ can be used

- to determine a project's rate of return or value. The time of _____s into and out of projects are used as inputs in financial models such as internal rate of return, and net present value.
- to determine problems with a business's liquidity. Being profitable does not necessarily mean being liquid. A company can fail because of a shortage of cash, even while profitable.
- as an alternate measure of a business's profits when it is believed that accrual accounting concepts do not represent economic realities. For example, a company may be notionally profitable but generating little operational cash (as may be the case for a company that barters its products rather than selling for cash.) In such a case, the company may be deriving additional operating cash by issuing shares evaluating default risk, re-investment requirements, etc.

_____ is a generic term used differently depending on the context. It may be defined by users for their own purposes.

Chapter 14. Strategic Issues in Making Investment Decisions

a. Gross profit
b. Gross profit margin
c. Sweat equity
d. Cash flow

5. _____ is the value on a given date of a future payment or series of future payments, discounted to reflect the time value of money and other factors such as investment risk. _____ calculations are widely used in business and economics to provide a means to compare cash flows at different times on a meaningful 'like to like' basis.

If offered a choice between $100 today or $100 in one year, everyone will choose $100 today.

a. Net present value
b. Discounted cash flow
c. Present value
d. 1990 Clean Air Act

6. _____ is a group creativity technique designed to generate a large number of ideas for the solution of a problem. The method was first popularized in the late 1930s by Alex Faickney Osborn in a book called Applied Imagination. Osborn proposed that groups could double their creative output with _____.
a. Brainstorming
b. Affiliation
c. Adam Smith
d. Abraham Harold Maslow

7. _____ is a term used for a number of concepts involving either the performance of an investigation of a business or person, or the performance of an act with a certain standard of care. It can be a legal obligation, but the term will more commonly apply to voluntary investigations. A common example of _____ in various industries is the process through which a potential acquirer evaluates a target company or its assets for acquisition.
a. Negligence in employment
b. Due diligence
c. Technology transfer
d. Flextime

8. In the fields of science, engineering, industry and statistics, _____ is the degree of closeness of a measured or calculated quantity to its actual (true) value. _____ is closely related to precision, also called reproducibility or repeatability, the degree to which further measurements or calculations show the same or similar results. _____ indicates proximity to the true value, precision to the repeatability or reproducibility of the measurement

The results of calculations or a measurement can be accurate but not precise, precise but not accurate, neither, or both.

a. A4e
b. AAAI
c. A Stake in the Outcome
d. Accuracy

9. A _____ is a professional who provides advice in a particular area of expertise such as management, accountancy, the environment, entertainment, technology, law , human resources, marketing, medicine, finance, economics, public affairs, communication, engineering, sound system design, graphic design, or waste management.

A _____ is usually an expert or a professional in a specific field and has a wide knowledge of the subject matter. A _____ usually works for a consultancy firm or is self-employed, and engages with multiple and changing clients.

Chapter 14. Strategic Issues in Making Investment Decisions   75

a. 33 Strategies of War
c. 1990 Clean Air Act
b. 28-hour day
d. Consultant

10. _____ is an organized social movement and market-based approach that aims to help producers in developing countries and promote sustainability. The movement advocates the payment of a higher price to producers as well as social and environmental standards in areas related to the production of a wide variety of goods. It focuses in particular on exports from developing countries to developed countries, most notably handicrafts, coffee, cocoa, sugar, tea, bananas, honey, cotton, wine, fresh fruit, chocolate and flowers.

a. 33 Strategies of War
c. 1990 Clean Air Act
b. 28-hour day
d. Fair trade

11. _____ is a strategic planning method that some organizations use to make flexible long-term plans. It is in large part an adaptation and generalization of classic methods used by military intelligence.

The original method was that a group of analysts would generate simulation games for policy makers. In business applications, the emphasis on gaming the behavior of opponents was reduced (shifting more toward a game against nature). At Royal Dutch/Shell for example, _____ was viewed as changing mindsets about the exogenous part of the world, prior to formulating specific strategies.

a. Retroactive overtime
c. Time and attendance
b. Labour productivity
d. Scenario planning

12. _____ is the study of how the variation (uncertainty) in the output of a mathematical model can be apportioned, qualitatively or quantitatively, to different sources of variation in the input of a model.

In more general terms uncertainty and sensitivity analyses investigate the robustness of a study when the study includes some form of mathematical modelling. While uncertainty analysis studies the overall uncertainty in the conclusions of the study, _____ tries to identify what source of uncertainty weights more on the study's conclusions.

a. No-bid contract
c. Foreign ownership
b. Policies and procedures
d. Sensitivity analysis

13. In probability theory and statistics, the _____ of a random variable is the integral of the random variable with respect to its probability measure. For discrete random variables this is equivalent to the probability-weighted sum of the possible values, and for continuous random variables with a density function it is the probability density -weighted integral of the possible values.

a. A4e
c. A Stake in the Outcome
b. AAAI
d. Expected value

14.

_____ is a systematic method to improve the 'value' of goods or products and services by using an examination of function. Value, as defined, is the ratio of function to cost. Value can therefore be increased by either improving the function or reducing the cost.

Chapter 14. Strategic Issues in Making Investment Decisions

a. Capacity planning
c. Cellular manufacturing
b. Master production schedule
d. Value engineering

15. In business and accounting, _____s are everything of value that is owned by a person or company. Any property or object of value that one possesses, usually considered as applicable to the payment of one's debts is considered an _____. Simplistically stated, _____s are things of value that can be readily converted into cash.
   a. A4e
   c. A Stake in the Outcome
   b. AAAI
   d. Asset

16. _____ can be regarded as an outcome of mental processes (cognitive process) leading to the selection of a course of action among several alternatives. Every _____ process produces a final choice. The output can be an action or an opinion of choice.
   a. 1990 Clean Air Act
   c. Decision making
   b. 28-hour day
   d. 33 Strategies of War

17. In economics, business, retail, and accounting, a _____ is the value of money that has been used up to produce something, and hence is not available for use anymore. In economics, a _____ is an alternative that is given up as a result of a decision. In business, the _____ may be one of acquisition, in which case the amount of money expended to acquire it is counted as _____.
   a. Cost
   c. Cost allocation
   b. Fixed costs
   d. Cost overrun

18. _____ is a process of attributing cost to particular cost centres. For example the wage of the driver of the purchasing department can be allocated to the purchasing department cost centre. It is not necessary to share the wage cost over several different cost centers.cost and services are not identical to each other.
   a. Cost accounting
   c. Cost overrun
   b. Fixed costs
   d. Cost allocation

19. In finance, an _____ is a contract between a buyer and a seller that gives the buyer the right--but not the obligation-- to buy or to sell a particular asset (the underlying asset) at a later day at an agreed price. In return for granting the _____, the seller collects a payment (the premium) from the buyer. A call _____ gives the buyer the right to buy the underlying asset; a put _____ gives the buyer of the _____ the right to sell the underlying asset.
   a. A Stake in the Outcome
   c. A4e
   b. Option
   d. AAAI

20. The general definition of an _____ is an evaluation of a person, organization, system, process, project or product. _____s are performed to ascertain the validity and reliability of information; also to provide an assessment of a system's internal control. The goal of an _____ is to express an opinion on the person / organization/system (etc) in question, under evaluation based on work done on a test basis.
   a. A Stake in the Outcome
   c. Audit committee
   b. Internal control
   d. Audit

Chapter 14. Strategic Issues in Making Investment Decisions

21. In accounting and auditing, _____ is defined as a process effected by an organization's structure, work and authority flows, people and management information systems, designed to help the organization accomplish specific goals or objectives. It is a means by which an organization's resources are directed, monitored, and measured. It plays an important role in preventing and detecting fraud and protecting the organization's resources, both physical (e.g., machinery and property) and intangible (e.g., reputation or intellectual property such as trademarks.)
   a. Audit committee
   b. A Stake in the Outcome
   c. Internal auditing
   d. Internal control

22. The _____ of 2002 (Pub.L. 107-204, 116 Stat. 745, enacted July 30, 2002), also known as the Public Company Accounting Reform and Investor Protection Act of 2002 and commonly called Sarbanes-Oxley, Sarbox or SOX, is a United States federal law enacted on July 30, 2002, as a reaction to a number of major corporate and accounting scandals including those affecting Enron, Tyco International, Adelphia, Peregrine Systems and WorldCom.
   a. Fair Labor Standards Act
   b. Letter of credit
   c. Sarbanes-Oxley Act
   d. Sarbanes-Oxley Act of 2002

23. The _____, also known as the Public Company Accounting Reform and Investor Protection Act of 2002 and commonly called Sarbanes-Oxley, Sarbox or SOX, is a United States federal law enacted on July 30, 2002, as a reaction to a number of major corporate and accounting scandals including those affecting Enron, Tyco International, Adelphia, Peregrine Systems and WorldCom.
   a. Sarbanes-Oxley Act of 2002
   b. MacPherson v. Buick Motor Co.
   c. Munn v. Illinois
   d. Letter of credit

24. _____ generally refers to a list of all planned expenses and revenues. It is a plan for saving and spending. A _____ is an important concept in microeconomics, which uses a _____ line to illustrate the trade-offs between two or more goods.
   a. Budget
   b. 28-hour day
   c. 33 Strategies of War
   d. 1990 Clean Air Act

25. _____ is one of the managerial functions like planning, organizing, staffing and directing. It is an important function because it helps to check the errors and to take the corrective action so that deviation from standards are minimized and stated goals of the organization are achieved in desired manner.According to modern concepts, _____ is a foreseeing action whereas earlier concept of _____ was used only when errors were detected. _____ in management means setting standards, measuring actual performance and taking corrective action.
   a. Control
   b. Schedule of reinforcement
   c. Turnover
   d. Decision tree pruning

26. The _____ is a rate of return used in capital budgeting to measure and compare the profitability of investments. It is also called the discounted cash flow rate of return (DCFROR) or simply the rate of return (ROR.) In the context of savings and loans the IRR is also called the effective interest rate.
   a. AAAI
   b. A4e
   c. Internal rate of return
   d. A Stake in the Outcome

27. _____ or economic opportunity loss is the value of the next best alternative forgone as the result of making a decision. _____ analysis is an important part of a company's decision-making processes but is not treated as an actual cost in any financial statement. The next best thing that a person can engage in is referred to as the _____ of doing the best thing and ignoring the next best thing to be done.

Chapter 14. Strategic Issues in Making Investment Decisions

a. A4e
b. A Stake in the Outcome
c. AAAI
d. Opportunity cost

28. _____ in business and economics refers to the period of time required for the return on an investment to 'repay' the sum of the original investment. For example, a $1000 investment which returned $500 per year would have a two year _____. It intuitively measures how long something takes to 'pay for itself.' Shorter _____s are obviously preferable to longer _____s (all else being equal.)
   a. Novated lease
   b. Net worth
   c. Market value
   d. Payback period

29. The _____ of an edge is $c_f(u, v) = c(u, v) - f(u, v)$. This defines a residual network denoted $G_f(V, E_f)$, giving the amount of available capacity. See that there can be an edge from u to v in the residual network, even though there is no edge from u to v in the original network.
   a. 1990 Clean Air Act
   b. 28-hour day
   c. 33 Strategies of War
   d. Residual capacity

30. In financial accounting, _____ , cash flow provided by operations or cash flow from operating activities, refers to the amount of cash a company generates from the revenues it brings in, excluding costs associated with long-term investment on capital items or investment in securities.

_____ = Cash generated from operations less taxation and interest paid, investment income received and less dividends paid gives rise to _____s per International Financial Reporting Standards.

To calculate cash generated from operations, one must calculate cash generated from customers and cash paid to suppliers.

   a. Operating cash flow
   b. A Stake in the Outcome
   c. AAAI
   d. A4e

31. In finance, _____, is the ratio of money gained or lost on an investment relative to the amount of money invested. The amount of money gained or lost may be referred to as interest, profit/loss, gain/loss, or net income/loss. The money invested may be referred to as the asset, capital, principal, or the cost basis of the investment.
   a. Rate of return
   b. Return on Capital Employed
   c. Return on sales
   d. Financial ratio

32. The _____ is an interest rate a central bank charges depository institutions that borrow reserves from it.

Chapter 14. Strategic Issues in Making Investment Decisions

The term _____ has two meanings:

- the same as interest rate; the term 'discount' does not refer to the meaning of the word, but to the purpose of using the quantity, such as computations of present value, e.g. net present value or discounted cash flow

- the annual effective _____, which is the annual interest divided by the capital including that interest; this rate is lower than the interest rate; it corresponds to using the value after a year as the nominal value, and seeing the initial value as the nominal value minus a discount; it is used for Treasury Bills and similar financial instruments

The annual effective _____ is the annual interest divided by the capital including that interest, which is the interest rate divided by 100% plus the interest rate. It is the annual discount factor to be applied to the future cash flow, to find the discount, subtracted from a future value to find the value one year earlier.

For example, suppose there is a government bond that sells for $95 and pays $100 in a year's time.

a. 28-hour day
c. 1990 Clean Air Act
b. Discount rate
d. 33 Strategies of War

33. The _____ is the interest rate that it is assumed can be obtained by investing in financial instruments with no default risk. However, the financial instrument can carry other types of risk, e.g. market risk (the risk of changes in market interest rates), liquidity risk (the risk of being unable to sell the instrument for cash at short notice without significant costs), etc.

Though a truly risk-free asset exists only in theory, in practice most professionals and academics use short-dated government bonds of the currency in question.

a. Risk-free interest rate
c. 33 Strategies of War
b. 1990 Clean Air Act
d. 28-hour day

34. In economics, _____ is a rise in the general level of prices of goods and services in an economy over a period of time. When the general price level rises, each unit of the functional currency buys fewer goods and services; consequently, _____ is a decline in the real value of money--a loss of purchasing power in the internal medium of exchange which is also the monetary unit of account in an economy. A chief measure of general price-level _____ is the general _____ rate, which is the percentage change in a general price index (normally the Consumer Price Index) over time.

a. Economy
c. A4e
b. A Stake in the Outcome
d. Inflation

35. _____ is a financial mechanism in which a debtor obtains the right to delay payments to a creditor, for a defined period of time, in exchange for a charge or fee. Essentially, the party that owes money in the present purchases the right to delay the payment until some future date. The discount, or charge, is simply the difference between the original amount owed in the present and the amount that has to be paid in the future to settle the debt.

a. Financial modeling
c. Linear model
b. Discounting
d. Ruin theory

Chapter 15. Budgeting and Financial Planning

1. _____ is a business Advocate term for an element which is necessary for an organization or project to achieve its mission. They are the critical factors or activities required for ensuring the success of your business. The term was initially used in the world of data analysis, and business analysis.

   a. Critical success factor
   b. Customer satisfaction
   c. Collaborative leadership
   d. Business hours

2. _____ is an organization's process of defining its strategy and making decisions on allocating its resources to pursue this strategy, including its capital and people. Various business analysis techniques can be used in _____, including SWOT analysis (Strengths, Weaknesses, Opportunities, and Threats) and PEST analysis (Political, Economic, Social, and Technological analysis) or STEER analysis involving Socio-cultural, Technological, Economic, Ecological, and Regulatory factors and EPISTEL (Environment, Political, Informatic, Social, Technological, Economic and Legal)

   _____ is the formal consideration of an organization's future course. All _____ deals with at least one of three key questions:

   1. 'What do we do?'
   2. 'For whom do we do it?'
   3. 'How do we excel?'

   In business _____, the third question is better phrased 'How can we beat or avoid competition?'. (Bradford and Duncan, page 1.)

   a. 1990 Clean Air Act
   b. 28-hour day
   c. 33 Strategies of War
   d. Strategic planning

3. _____ is, in very basic words, a position a firm occupies against its competitors.

   According to Michael Porter, the three methods for creating a sustainable _____ are through:

   1. Cost leadership

   2. Differentiation

   3. Focus (economics)

   a. 28-hour day
   b. 1990 Clean Air Act
   c. Theory Z
   d. Competitive advantage

4. _____ generally refers to a list of all planned expenses and revenues. It is a plan for saving and spending. A _____ is an important concept in microeconomics, which uses a _____ line to illustrate the trade-offs between two or more goods.

   a. 28-hour day
   b. 1990 Clean Air Act
   c. 33 Strategies of War
   d. Budget

5. In economics, business, retail, and accounting, a _____ is the value of money that has been used up to produce something, and hence is not available for use anymore. In economics, a _____ is an alternative that is given up as a result of a decision. In business, the _____ may be one of acquisition, in which case the amount of money expended to acquire it is counted as _____.
   a. Fixed costs
   b. Cost allocation
   c. Cost overrun
   d. Cost

6. _____ is the process whereby companies use cost accounting to report or control the various costs of doing business.

   _____ generally describes the approaches and activities of managers in short run and long run planning and control decisions that increase value for customers and lower costs of products and services.

   a. Cost Management
   b. Genbutsu
   c. Strict liability
   d. Missing completely at random

7. _____, in strategic management and marketing is, according to Carlton O'Neal, the percentage or proportion of the total available market or market segment that is being serviced by a company. It can be expressed as a company's sales revenue (from that market) divided by the total sales revenue available in that market. It can also be expressed as a company's unit sales volume (in a market) divided by the total volume of units sold in that market.
   a. Green marketing
   b. Marketing plan
   c. Business-to-business
   d. Market share

8. _____ is used to assign the available resources in an economic way. It is part of resource management.

   In strategic planning,is a plan for using available resources, for example human resources, especially in the near term, to achieve goals for the future.

   a. Resource allocation
   b. 1990 Clean Air Act
   c. 33 Strategies of War
   d. 28-hour day

9. _____ is one of the managerial functions like planning, organizing, staffing and directing. It is an important function because it helps to check the errors and to take the corrective action so that deviation from standards are minimized and stated goals of the organization are achieved in desired manner. According to modern concepts, _____ is a foreseeing action whereas earlier concept of _____ was used only when errors were detected. _____ in management means setting standards, measuring actual performance and taking corrective action.
   a. Control
   b. Turnover
   c. Schedule of reinforcement
   d. Decision tree pruning

10. _____ is the planning process used to determine whether a firm's long term investments such as new machinery, replacement machinery, new plants, new products, and research development projects are worth pursuing. It is budget for major capital, or investment, expenditures.

Many formal methods are used in _____, including the techniques such as

- Net present value
- Profitability index
- Internal rate of return
- Modified Internal Rate of Return
- Equivalent annuity

These methods use the incremental cash flows from each potential investment, or project. Techniques based on accounting earnings and accounting rules are sometimes used - though economists consider this to be improper - such as the accounting rate of return, and 'return on investment.' Simplified and hybrid methods are used as well, such as payback period and discounted payback period.

a. Gross profit
c. Gross profit margin
b. Restricted stock
d. Capital budgeting

11. In probability theory, a probability distribution is called _____ if its cumulative distribution function is _____. This is equivalent to saying that for random variables X with the distribution in question, Pr[X = a] = 0 for all real numbers a, i.e.: the probability that X attains the value a is zero, for any number a. If the distribution of X is _____ then X is called a _____ random variable.

a. Pay Band
c. Connectionist expert systems
b. Decision tree pruning
d. Continuous

12. In economics and sociology, an _____ is any factor (financial or non-financial) that enables or motivates a particular course of action, or counts as a reason for preferring one choice to the alternatives. It is an expectation that encourages people to behave in a certain way. Since human beings are purposeful creatures, the study of _____ structures is central to the study of all economic activity (both in terms of individual decision-making and in terms of co-operation and competition within a larger institutional structure.)

a. A4e
c. A Stake in the Outcome
b. AAAI
d. Incentive

13. _____ is a company's financial statement that indicates how the revenue is transformed into the net income The purpose of the _____ is to show managers and investors whether the company made or lost money during the period being reported.

The important thing to remember about an _____ is that it represents a period of time.

a. A4e
c. A Stake in the Outcome
b. Income statement
d. AAAI

14. _____ are formal records of the financial activities of a business, person, or other entity. In British English, including United Kingdom company law, _____ are often referred to as accounts, although the term _____ is also used, particularly by accountants.

_____ provide an overview of a business or person's financial condition in both short and long term.

Chapter 15. Budgeting and Financial Planning

a. 28-hour day
c. 1990 Clean Air Act
b. 33 Strategies of War
d. Financial statements

15. The _____ is a systematic, interactive forecasting method which relies on a panel of independent experts. The carefully selected experts answer questionnaires in two or more rounds. After each round, a facilitator provides an anonymous summary of the experts' forecasts from the previous round as well as the reasons they provided for their judgments.

a. Hoshin Kanri
c. Delphi method
b. Quality function deployment
d. Learning organization

16. _____ is the process of estimation in unknown situations. Prediction is a similar, but more general term. Both can refer to estimation of time series, cross-sectional or longitudinal data.

a. Forecasting
c. 33 Strategies of War
b. 1990 Clean Air Act
d. 28-hour day

17. The term '_____' refers to the concept of collecting information and attempting to spot a pattern in the information. In some fields of study, the term '_____' has more formally-defined meanings.

In project management _____ is a mathematical technique that uses historical results to predict future outcome.

a. Regression analysis
c. Least squares
b. Stepwise regression
d. Trend analysis

18. _____s are statistical models used in econometrics. An _____ specifies the statistical relationship that is believed to hold between the various economic quantities pertaining a particular economic phenomena under study. An _____ can be derived from a deterministic economic model by allowing for uncertainty or from an economic model which itself is stochastic.

a. AAAI
c. A4e
b. A Stake in the Outcome
d. Econometric model

19. _____ of the learning curve effect and the closely related experience curve effect express the relationship between equations for experience and efficiency or between efficiency gains and investment in the effort. The experience of 'learning curves' was first observed by the 19th Century German psychologist Hermann Ebbinghaus according to the difficulty of memorizing varying numbers of verbal stimuli, and subsequent learning about the complex processes of learning are discussed in the

The rule used for representing the learning curve effect states that the more times a task has been performed, the less time will be required on each subsequent iteration.

a. Distribution
c. Spatial Decision Support Systems
b. Point biserial correlation coefficient
d. Models

Chapter 15. Budgeting and Financial Planning

20. The phrase _____, according to the Organization for Economic Co-operation and Development, refers to 'creative work undertaken on a systematic basis in order to increase the stock of knowledge, including knowledge of man, culture and society, and the use of this stock of knowledge to devise new applications [sic]'

New product design and development is more than often a crucial factor in the survival of a company. In an industry that is fast changing, firms must continually revise their design and range of products. This is necessary due to continuous technology change and development as well as other competitors and the changing preference of customers.

a. 1990 Clean Air Act
c. Research and development
b. 28-hour day
d. 33 Strategies of War

21. _____ is an advertisement in which a particular product specifically mentions a competitor by name for the express purpose of showing why the competitor is inferior to the product naming it.

This should not be confused with parody advertisements, where a fictional product is being advertised for the purpose of poking fun at the particular advertisement, nor should it be confused with the use of a coined brand name for the purpose of comparing the product without actually naming an actual competitor. ('Wikipedia tastes better and is less filling than the Encyclopedia Galactica.')

In the 1980s, during what has been referred to as the cola wars, soft-drink manufacturer Pepsi ran a series of advertisements where people, caught on hidden camera, in a blind taste test, chose Pepsi over rival Coca-Cola.

a. 1990 Clean Air Act
c. 33 Strategies of War
b. 28-hour day
d. Comparative advertising

22. _____ is a costing model that identifies activities in an organization and assigns the cost of each activity resource to all products and services according to the actual consumption by each: it assigns more indirect costs (overhead) into direct costs.

In this way an organization can establish the true cost of its individual products and services for the purposes of identifying and eliminating those which are unprofitable and lowering the prices of those which are overpriced.

In a business organization, the ABC methodology assigns an organization's resource costs through activities to the products and services provided to its customers.

a. A4e
c. A Stake in the Outcome
b. Indirect costs
d. Activity-based costing

23. A _____ is a process in which a potential employee is evaluated by an employer for prospective employment in their company, organization and was established in the late 16th century.

A _____ typically precedes the hiring decision, and is used to evaluate the candidate. The interview is usually preceded by the evaluation of submitted résumés from interested candidates, then selecting a small number of candidates for interviews.

Chapter 15. Budgeting and Financial Planning

a. Supported employment
c. Split shift
b. Payrolling
d. Job interview

24. In economics, _____ is a rise in the general level of prices of goods and services in an economy over a period of time. When the general price level rises, each unit of the functional currency buys fewer goods and services; consequently, _____ is a decline in the real value of money--a loss of purchasing power in the internal medium of exchange which is also the monetary unit of account in an economy. A chief measure of general price-level _____ is the general _____ rate, which is the percentage change in a general price index (normally the Consumer Price Index) over time.
a. Economy
c. A4e
b. A Stake in the Outcome
d. Inflation

25. In economics, _____ are business expenses that are not dependent on the activities of the business They tend to be time-related, such as salaries or rents being paid per month. This is in contrast to variable costs, which are volume-related (and are paid per quantity.)

In management accounting, _____ are defined as expenses that do not change in proportion to the activity of a business, within the relevant period or scale of production.

a. Fixed costs
c. Cost allocation
b. Cost of quality
d. Transaction cost

26. _____s are expenses that change in proportion to the activity of a business. In other words, _____ is the sum of marginal costs. It can also be considered normal costs.
a. Cost overrun
c. Variable cost
b. Cost accounting
d. Fixed costs

27. Total _____ is a method of Accounting cost which entails the full cost of manufacturing or providing a service. This includes not just the costs of materials and labour, but also of all manufacturing overheads (whether 'fixed' or 'variable'.) One of the main reasons for absorbing overheads into the cost of units is for inventory valuation purposes.
a. A4e
c. Absorption costing
b. AAAI
d. A Stake in the Outcome

28. In financial accounting, a _____ or statement of financial position is a summary of a person's or organization's balances. Assets, liabilities and ownership equity are listed as of a specific date, such as the end of its financial year. A _____ is often described as a snapshot of a company's financial condition.
a. 28-hour day
c. Balance sheet
b. 33 Strategies of War
d. 1990 Clean Air Act

29. A _____ is the belief that there is a technique, method, process, activity, incentive or reward that is more effective at delivering a particular outcome than any other technique, method, process, etc. The idea is that with proper processes, checks, and testing, a desired outcome can be delivered with fewer problems and unforeseen complications. _____s can also be defined as the most efficient (least amount of effort) and effective (best results) way of accomplishing a task, based on repeatable procedures that have proven themselves over time for large numbers of people.
a. Design management
c. Hierarchical organization
b. Fix it twice
d. Best practice

Chapter 15. Budgeting and Financial Planning

30. _____ is the level of inventory that minimizes the total inventory holding costs and ordering costs. The framework used to determine this order quantity is also known as Wilson _____ Model. The model was developed by F. W. Harris in 1913.
   a. Event management
   c. Anti-leadership
   b. Effective executive
   d. Economic order quantity

31. In business management, _____ is money spent to keep and maintain a stock of goods in storage.

The most obvious _____s include rent for the required space; equipment, materials, and labor to operate the space; insurance; security; interest on money invested in the inventory and space, and other direct expenses. Some stored goods become obsolete before they are sold, reducing their contribution to revenue while having no effect on their _____.

   a. Private placement
   c. Market niche
   b. Choquet integral
   d. Holding cost

32. _____ is an inventory strategy that strives to improve the return on investment of a business by reducing in-process inventory and its associated carrying costs. To meet _____ objectives, the process relies on signals between different points in the process. This means the process is often driven by a series of signals, or Kanban , which tell production when to make the next part. Kanban are usually 'tickets' but can be simple visual signals, such as the presence or absence of a part on a shelf. Implemented correctly, _____ can dramatically improve a manufacturing organization's return on investment, quality, and efficiency.
   a. 33 Strategies of War
   c. 28-hour day
   b. Just-in-time
   d. 1990 Clean Air Act

33. A _____ is the period of time between the initiation of any process of production and the completion of that process. Thus the _____ for ordering a new car from a manufacturer may be anywhere from 2 weeks to 6 months. In industry, _____ reduction is an important part of lean manufacturing.
   a. Lead time
   c. 1990 Clean Air Act
   b. 33 Strategies of War
   d. 28-hour day

34. _____ is a term used by inventory specialists to describe a level of extra stock that is maintained below the cycle stock to buffer against stockouts. _____ exists to counter uncertainties in supply and demand. _____ is defined as extra units of inventory carried as protection against possible stockouts .(shortfall in raw material or packaging.)
   a. Knowledge worker
   c. Product life cycle
   b. Safety stock
   d. Process automation

Chapter 16. Standard Costing, Variance Analysis, and Kaizen Costing

1. _____ is one of the managerial functions like planning, organizing, staffing and directing. It is an important function because it helps to check the errors and to take the corrective action so that deviation from standards are minimized and stated goals of the organization are achieved in desired manner. According to modern concepts, _____ is a foreseeing action whereas earlier concept of _____ was used only when errors were detected. _____ in management means setting standards, measuring actual performance and taking corrective action.

   a. Decision tree pruning
   b. Turnover
   c. Control
   d. Schedule of reinforcement

2. In economics, business, retail, and accounting, a _____ is the value of money that has been used up to produce something, and hence is not available for use anymore. In economics, a _____ is an alternative that is given up as a result of a decision. In business, the _____ may be one of acquisition, in which case the amount of money expended to acquire it is counted as _____.

   a. Fixed costs
   b. Cost overrun
   c. Cost allocation
   d. Cost

3. _____ is a 'policy by which management devotes its time to investigating only those situations in which actual results differ significantly from planned results. The idea is that management should spend its valuable time concentrating on the more important items (such as shaping the company's future strategic course.) Attention is given only to material deviations requiring investigation.'

   It is not entirely synonymous with the concept of exception management in that it describes a policy where absolute focus is on exception management, in contrast to moderate application of exception management.

   a. Trustee
   b. C-A-K-E
   c. Management by exception
   d. Business philosophy

4. _____ is the analysis of how a task is accomplished, including a detailed description of both manual and mental activities, task and element durations, task frequency, task allocation, task complexity, environmental conditions, necessary clothing and equipment, and any other unique factors involved in or required for one or more people to perform a given task. _____ emerged from research in applied behavior analysis and still has considerable research in that area.

   Information from a _____ can then be used for many purposes, such as personnel selection and training, tool or equipment design, procedure design (e.g., design of checklists or decision support systems) and automation.

   a. 28-hour day
   b. 33 Strategies of War
   c. 1990 Clean Air Act
   d. Task analysis

5. The term '_____' refers to the concept of collecting information and attempting to spot a pattern in the information. In some fields of study, the term '_____' has more formally-defined meanings.

   In project management _____ is a mathematical technique that uses historical results to predict future outcome.

   a. Trend analysis
   b. Stepwise regression
   c. Least squares
   d. Regression analysis

Chapter 16. Standard Costing, Variance Analysis, and Kaizen Costing

6. In differential topology, a _____ of a differentiable function between differentiable manifolds is the image of a critical point.

The basic result on _____s is Sard's lemma. The set of _____s can be quite irregular; but in Morse theory it becomes important to consider real-valued functions on a manifold M, such that the set of _____s is in fact finite.

a. Critical value
c. 1990 Clean Air Act
b. 33 Strategies of War
d. 28-hour day

7. The _____ in statistical process control is a tool used to determine whether a manufacturing or business process is in a state of statistical control or not.

If the chart indicates that the process is currently under control then it can be used with confidence to predict the future performance of the process. If the chart indicates that the process being monitored is not in control, the pattern it reveals can help determine the source of variation to be eliminated to bring the process back into control.

a. Simple moving average
c. Failure rate
b. Control chart
d. Time series analysis

8. A _____ is an employee within a company, business or other organization who is responsible at some level for buying or approving the acquisition of goods and services needed by the company. The position responsibilities may be the same as that of a buyer or purchasing agent, or may include wider supervisory or managerial responsibilities. A _____ may oversee the acquisition of materials needed for production, general supplies for offices and facilities, equipment, or construction contracts.

a. Financial analyst
c. Purchasing manager
b. CEO
d. Director of communications

9. The _____ is a concept from business management that was first described and popularized by Michael Porter in his 1985 best-seller, Competitive Advantage: Creating and Sustaining Superior Performance.

A _____ is a chain of activities. Products pass through all activities of the chain in order and at each activity the product gains some value. The chain of activities gives the products more added value than the sum of added values of all activities. It is important not to mix the concept of the _____ with the costs occurring throughout the activities.

a. Market development
c. Value chain
b. Mass marketing
d. Customer relationship management

10. The _____ of an edge is $c_f(u, v) = c(u, v) - f(u, v)$. This defines a residual network denoted $G_f(V, E_f)$, giving the amount of available capacity. See that there can be an edge from u to v in the residual network, even though there is no edge from u to v in the original network.

a. 1990 Clean Air Act
b. 28-hour day
c. 33 Strategies of War
d. Residual capacity

11. A barcode (also bar code) is an optical machine-readable representation of data. Originally, _____ represented data in the widths (lines) and the spacings of parallel lines, and may be referred to as linear or 1D (1 dimensional) barcodes or symbologies. They also come in patterns of squares, dots, hexagons and other geometric patterns within images termed 2D (2 dimensional) matrix codes or symbologies.
a. 1990 Clean Air Act
b. 28-hour day
c. 33 Strategies of War
d. Bar codes

12. _____ is a method of identifying and evaluating activities that a business performs using activity-based costing to carry out a value chain analysis or a re-engineering initiative to improve strategic and operational decisions in an organization. Activity-based costing establishes relationships between overhead costs and activities so that overhead costs can be more precisely allocated to products, services, or customer segments. _____ focuses on managing activities to reduce costs and improve customer value.
a. Indirect costs
b. A4e
c. A Stake in the Outcome
d. Activity-based management

13. In economics, and cost accounting, _____ describes the total economic cost of production and is made up of variable costs, which vary according to the quantity of a good produced and include inputs such as labor and raw materials, plus fixed costs, which are independent of the quantity of a good produced and include inputs (capital) that cannot be varied in the short term, such as buildings and machinery. _____ in economics includes the total opportunity cost of each factor of production in addition to fixed and variable costs.

The rate at which _____ changes as the amount produced changes is called marginal cost.

a. 28-hour day
b. 33 Strategies of War
c. 1990 Clean Air Act
d. Total cost

14. _____ is a financial estimate designed to help consumers and enterprise managers assess direct and indirect costs It is a form of full cost accounting.
a. 1990 Clean Air Act
b. Total cost of ownership
c. 33 Strategies of War
d. 28-hour day

15. _____ is, in very basic words, a position a firm occupies against its competitors.

According to Michael Porter, the three methods for creating a sustainable _____ are through:

1. Cost leadership

2. Differentiation

3. Focus (economics)

Chapter 16. Standard Costing, Variance Analysis, and Kaizen Costing

    a. 28-hour day
    b. 1990 Clean Air Act
    c. Competitive advantage
    d. Theory Z

16. _____ is the state or fact of exclusive rights and control over property, which may be an object, land/real estate or intellectual property. An _____ right is also referred to as title. The concept of _____ has existed for thousands of years and in all cultures.
    a. Emanation of the state
    b. A4e
    c. A Stake in the Outcome
    d. Ownership

17. _____ are conventions, treaties and recommendations designed to eliminate unjust and inhumane labour practices. The primary inernational agency charged with developing such standards is the International Labour Organization (ILO.) Established in 1919, the ILO advocates international standards as essential for the eradication of labour conditions involving 'injustice, hardship and privation'.
    a. Airbus Industrie
    b. International labour standards
    c. Anaconda Copper
    d. Airbus SAS

18. A _____ is a special type of bar chart where the values being plotted are arranged in descending order. The graph is accompanied by a line graph which shows the cumulative totals of each category, left to right. The chart was named for Vilfredo Pareto.
    a. 28-hour day
    b. 1990 Clean Air Act
    c. 33 Strategies of War
    d. Pareto chart

19. _____ Management is the succession of strategies used by management as a product goes through its _____. The conditions in which a product is sold changes over time and must be managed as it moves through its succession of stages.

The _____ goes through many phases, involves many professional disciplines, and requires many skills, tools and processes.

    a. Golden handshake
    b. Product life cycle
    c. Strategic Alliance
    d. Job hunting

20. _____ is a business management strategy aimed at embedding awareness of quality in all organizational processes. _____ has been widely used in manufacturing, education, hospitals, call centers, government, and service industries, as well as NASA space and science programs.

As defined by the International Organization for Standardization (ISO):

> '_____ is a management approach for an organization, centered on quality, based on the participation of all its members and aiming at long-term success through customer satisfaction, and benefits to all members of the organization and to society.' ISO 8402:1994

One major aim is to reduce variation from every process so that greater consistency of effort is obtained. (Royse, D., Thyer, B., Padgett D., ' Logan T., 2006)

a. 28-hour day
b. 1990 Clean Air Act
c. Quality management
d. Total quality management

21. A _____ is typically described as a deliberate plan of action to guide decisions and achieve rational outcome(s.) However, the term may also be used to denote what is actually done, even though it is unplanned.

The term may apply to government, private sector organizations and groups, and individuals.

a. 1990 Clean Air Act
b. 28-hour day
c. 33 Strategies of War
d. Policy

22. _____ can be considered to have three main components: quality control, quality assurance and quality improvement. _____ is focused not only on product quality, but also the means to achieve it. _____ therefore uses quality assurance and control of processes as well as products to achieve more consistent quality.

a. 28-hour day
b. Total quality management
c. 1990 Clean Air Act
d. Quality management

23. _____ is the process of comparing the cost, cycle time, productivity, or quality of a specific process or method to another that is widely considered to be an industry standard or best practice. Essentially, _____ provides a snapshot of the performance of your business and helps you understand where you are in relation to a particular standard. The result is often a business case for making changes in order to make improvements.

a. Benchmarking
b. Complementors
c. Cost leadership
d. Competitive heterogeneity

24. _____ in engineering is a method of manufacturing in which the entire production process is controlled by computer. The traditional separated process methods are joined through a computer by CIM. This integration allows that the processes exchange information with each other and they are able to initiate actions.

a. 33 Strategies of War
b. 1990 Clean Air Act
c. 28-hour day
d. Computer-integrated manufacturing

25. _____ is a Japanese philosophy that focuses on continuous improvement throughout all aspects of life. When applied to the workplace, _____ activities continually improve all functions of a business, from manufacturing to management and from the CEO to the assembly line workers. By improving standardized activities and processes, _____ aims to eliminate waste .

a. Sensitivity analysis
b. Psychological pricing
c. Cross-docking
d. Kaizen

26. _____ is an advertisement in which a particular product specifically mentions a competitor by name for the express purpose of showing why the competitor is inferior to the product naming it.

This should not be confused with parody advertisements, where a fictional product is being advertised for the purpose of poking fun at the particular advertisement, nor should it be confused with the use of a coined brand name for the purpose of comparing the product without actually naming an actual competitor. ('Wikipedia tastes better and is less filling than the Encyclopedia Galactica.')

Chapter 16. Standard Costing, Variance Analysis, and Kaizen Costing

In the 1980s, during what has been referred to as the cola wars, soft-drink manufacturer Pepsi ran a series of advertisements where people, caught on hidden camera, in a blind taste test, chose Pepsi over rival Coca-Cola.

a. 1990 Clean Air Act
b. 28-hour day
c. 33 Strategies of War
d. Comparative advertising

27. _____ is a costing model that identifies activities in an organization and assigns the cost of each activity resource to all products and services according to the actual consumption by each: it assigns more indirect costs (overhead) into direct costs.

In this way an organization can establish the true cost of its individual products and services for the purposes of identifying and eliminating those which are unprofitable and lowering the prices of those which are overpriced.

In a business organization, the ABC methodology assigns an organization's resource costs through activities to the products and services provided to its customers.

a. Indirect costs
b. Activity-based costing
c. A Stake in the Outcome
d. A4e

Chapter 17. Flexible Budgets, Overhead Cost Management, and Activity-Based Budgeting

1. _____ generally refers to a list of all planned expenses and revenues. It is a plan for saving and spending. A _____ is an important concept in microeconomics, which uses a _____ line to illustrate the trade-offs between two or more goods.
   - a. 28-hour day
   - b. 33 Strategies of War
   - c. Budget
   - d. 1990 Clean Air Act

2. _____ consists of the mental process of thinking involved with the process of judging the merits of multiple options and selecting one of them for action. Some simple examples include deciding whether to get up in the morning or go back to sleep, or selecting a given route for a journey. More complex examples (often decisions that affect what a person thinks or their core beliefs) include choosing a lifestyle, religious affiliation, or political position.
   - a. Championship mobilization
   - b. Groups decision making
   - c. Trade study
   - d. Choice

3. _____ in engineering is a method of manufacturing in which the entire production process is controlled by computer. The traditional separated process methods are joined through a computer by CIM. This integration allows that the processes exchange information with each other and they are able to initiate actions.
   - a. 28-hour day
   - b. 33 Strategies of War
   - c. 1990 Clean Air Act
   - d. Computer-integrated manufacturing

4. In business, overhead, _____ or overhead expense refers to an ongoing expense of operating a business. The term overhead is usually used to group expenses that are necessary to the continued functioning of the business, but do not directly generate profits.

Overhead expenses are all costs on the income statement except for direct labor and direct materials.

   - a. Interlocking directorate
   - b. Industrial market segmentation
   - c. Intangible assets
   - d. Overhead cost

5. In economics, business, retail, and accounting, a _____ is the value of money that has been used up to produce something, and hence is not available for use anymore. In economics, a _____ is an alternative that is given up as a result of a decision. In business, the _____ may be one of acquisition, in which case the amount of money expended to acquire it is counted as _____.
   - a. Cost overrun
   - b. Cost allocation
   - c. Cost
   - d. Fixed costs

6. _____ is, in very basic words, a position a firm occupies against its competitors.

According to Michael Porter, the three methods for creating a sustainable _____ are through:

1. Cost leadership

2. Differentiation

3. Focus (economics)

Chapter 17. Flexible Budgets, Overhead Cost Management, and Activity-Based Budgeting

a. 28-hour day
b. Theory Z
c. 1990 Clean Air Act
d. Competitive advantage

7. _____ is the process whereby companies use cost accounting to report or control the various costs of doing business.

_____ generally describes the approaches and activities of managers in short run and long run planning and control decisions that increase value for customers and lower costs of products and services.

a. Missing completely at random
b. Cost management
c. Genbutsu
d. Strict liability

8. _____ is a concept in economics which refers to the extent to which an enterprise or a nation actually uses its installed productive capacity. Thus, it refers to the relationship between actual output that 'is' produced with the installed equipment and the potential output which 'could' be produced with it, if capacity was fully used.

If market demand grows, _____ will rise.

a. Diseconomies of scale
b. Factors of production
c. Multifactor productivity
d. Capacity utilization

9. In queueing theory, _____ is the proportion of the system's resources which is used by the traffic which arrives at it. It should be strictly less than one for the system to function well. It is usually represented by the symbol ρ.

a. A4e
b. Utilization
c. A Stake in the Outcome
d. AAAI

10. Government _____ are designed to show nonfinancial aspects of government operations. For example, a government financial report might include the number of arrests, number of convictions by crime category as well as the change (i.e., increase or decrease) in crime rate. Government _____ usually provide data on environmental conditions, education and conditions of streets and roads.

a. 1990 Clean Air Act
b. Privatization
c. 28-hour day
d. Performance reports

11. _____ is a costing model that identifies activities in an organization and assigns the cost of each activity resource to all products and services according to the actual consumption by each: it assigns more indirect costs (overhead) into direct costs.

In this way an organization can establish the true cost of its individual products and services for the purposes of identifying and eliminating those which are unprofitable and lowering the prices of those which are overpriced.

In a business organization, the ABC methodology assigns an organization's resource costs through activities to the products and services provided to its customers.

a. Activity-based costing
b. A Stake in the Outcome
c. Indirect costs
d. A4e

Chapter 17. Flexible Budgets, Overhead Cost Management, and Activity-Based Budgeting

12. _____ is an inventory strategy that strives to improve the return on investment of a business by reducing in-process inventory and its associated carrying costs. To meet _____ objectives, the process relies on signals between different points in the process. This means the process is often driven by a series of signals, or Kanban, which tell production when to make the next part. Kanban are usually 'tickets' but can be simple visual signals, such as the presence or absence of a part on a shelf. Implemented correctly, _____ can dramatically improve a manufacturing organization's return on investment, quality, and efficiency.
   a. 1990 Clean Air Act
   b. 28-hour day
   c. 33 Strategies of War
   d. Just-in-time

13. _____ is an adverb or adjective, meaning in proportion. The term is used in many legal and economic contexts, and sometimes spelled pro-rata.

More specifically, _____ means:

   1. In proportion to some factor that can be exactly calculated.
   2. To count based on amount of time that has passed out of the total time.
   3. Proportional Ratio

Pro-rata has a Latin etymology, from pro, according to, for, or by, and rata, feminine ablative of calculated.

Examples in law and economics include the following noted below.

   a. 1990 Clean Air Act
   b. 33 Strategies of War
   c. 28-hour day
   d. Pro rata

14. In management accounting, _____ establishes budget and actual cost of operations, processes, departments or product and the analysis of variances, profitability or social use of funds. Managers use _____ to support decision-making to cut a company's costs and improve profitability. As a form of management accounting, _____ need not follow standards such as GAAP, because its primary use is for internal managers, rather than outside users, and what to compute is instead decided pragmatically.
   a. Quality costs
   b. Cost Accounting
   c. Marginal cost
   d. Transaction cost

15. In financial accounting, _____ or cost of sales includes the direct costs attributable to the production of the goods sold by a company. This amount includes the materials cost used in creating the goods along with the direct labour costs used to produce the good. It excludes indirect expenses such as distribution costs and sales force costs.
   a. 28-hour day
   b. Cost of goods sold
   c. Reorder point
   d. 1990 Clean Air Act

16. In cost-volume-profit analysis, a form of management accounting, _____ is the marginal profit per unit sale. It is a useful quantity in carrying out various calculations, and can be used as a measure of operating leverage.

The Total _____ is Total Revenue (TR, or Sales) minus Total Variable Cost (TVC):

$$TContribution\ margin = TR - TVC$$

Chapter 17. Flexible Budgets, Overhead Cost Management, and Activity-Based Budgeting

The Unit _____ (C) is Unit Revenue (Price, P) minus Unit Variable Cost (V):

$$C = P - V$$

The _____ Ratio is the percentage of Contribution over Total Revenue, which can be calculated from the unit contribution over unit price or total contribution over Total Revenue:

$$\frac{C}{P} = \frac{P - V}{P} = \frac{\text{Unit Contribution Margin}}{\text{Price}} = \frac{\text{Total Contribution Margin}}{\text{Total Revenue}}$$

For instance, if the price is $10 and the unit variable cost is $2, then the unit _____ is $8, and the _____ ratio is $8/$10 = 80%.

a. Factory overhead
b. Contribution margin
c. Profit center
d. Customer profitability

17. _____s are expenses that change in proportion to the activity of a business. In other words, _____ is the sum of marginal costs. It can also be considered normal costs.

a. Cost accounting
b. Fixed costs
c. Cost overrun
d. Variable cost

Chapter 18. Organizational Design, Responsibility Accounting, and Evaluation

1. _____ is the process by which the activities of an organisation, particularly those regarding decision-making, become concentrated within a particular location and/or group.
   a. Chief operating officer
   b. Product innovation
   c. Centralization
   d. Corner office

2. _____ is the process of dispersing decision-making governance closer to the people or citizen. It includes the dispersal of administration or governance in sectors or areas like engineering, management science, political science, political economy, sociology and economics. _____ is also possible in the dispersal of population and employment.
   a. Formula for Change
   b. Decentralization
   c. Business plan
   d. Frenemy

3. _____ refers to increasing the spiritual, political, social or economic strength of individuals and communities. It often involves the empowered developing confidence in their own capacities.

   The term Human _____ covers a vast landscape of meanings, interpretations, definitions and disciplines ranging from psychology and philosophy to the highly commercialized Self-Help industry and Motivational sciences.

   a. AAAI
   b. A Stake in the Outcome
   c. A4e
   d. Empowerment

4. In economics, business, retail, and accounting, a _____ is the value of money that has been used up to produce something, and hence is not available for use anymore. In economics, a _____ is an alternative that is given up as a result of a decision. In business, the _____ may be one of acquisition, in which case the amount of money expended to acquire it is counted as _____.
   a. Cost overrun
   b. Cost allocation
   c. Fixed costs
   d. Cost

5. _____s are parts of a corporation that directly add to its profit.

   A _____ manager is held accountable for both revenues, and costs (expenses), and therefore, profits. What this means in terms of managerial responsibilities is that the manager has to drive the sales revenue generating activities which leads to cash inflows and at the same time control the cost (cash outflows) causing activities.

   a. Customer profitability
   b. Process costing
   c. Profit center
   d. Factory overhead

6. _____ represents the total cash investment that shareholders and debtholders have made in a company. There are two different but completely equivalent methods for calculating _____. The operating approach is calculated as:

   _____ = Operating Net Working Capital + Net PP'E + Capitalized Operating Leases + Other Operating Assets + Operating Intangibles - Other Operating Liabilities - Cumulative Adjustment for Amortization of R'D

   Equivalently, the financing approach is calculated as:

Chapter 18. Organizational Design, Responsibility Accounting, and Evaluation

In symbols:

$$K = D + E - M$$

_____ is used in several important measurements of financial performance, including return on _____, economic value added, and free cash flow.

a. AAAI
c. A4e
b. A Stake in the Outcome
d. Invested capital

7. _____ is a 'policy by which management devotes its time to investigating only those situations in which actual results differ significantly from planned results. The idea is that management should spend its valuable time concentrating on the more important items (such as shaping the company's future strategic course.) Attention is given only to material deviations requiring investigation.'

It is not entirely synonymous with the concept of exception management in that it describes a policy where absolute focus is on exception management, in contrast to moderate application of exception management.

a. C-A-K-E
c. Trustee
b. Business philosophy
d. Management by exception

8. Government _____ are designed to show nonfinancial aspects of government operations. For example, a government financial report might include the number of arrests, number of convictions by crime category as well as the change (i.e., increase or decrease) in crime rate. Government _____ usually provide data on environmental conditions, education and conditions of streets and roads.

a. 1990 Clean Air Act
c. Performance reports
b. Privatization
d. 28-hour day

9. _____ generally refers to a list of all planned expenses and revenues. It is a plan for saving and spending. A _____ is an important concept in microeconomics, which uses a _____ line to illustrate the trade-offs between two or more goods.

a. 28-hour day
c. 1990 Clean Air Act
b. 33 Strategies of War
d. Budget

10. _____ are formal records of the financial activities of a business, person, or other entity. In British English, including United Kingdom company law, _____ are often referred to as accounts, although the term _____ is also used, particularly by accountants.

_____ provide an overview of a business or person's financial condition in both short and long term.

a. 28-hour day
c. 1990 Clean Air Act
b. 33 Strategies of War
d. Financial statements

Chapter 18. Organizational Design, Responsibility Accounting, and Evaluation

11. _____ is the process whereby an organization establishes the parameters within which programs, investments, and acquisitions are reaching the desired results. Performance Reference Model of the Federal Enterprise Architecture, 2005.

This process of measuring performance often requires the use of statistical evidence to determine progress toward specific defined organizational objectives.

There are many types of measurements.

    a. Crisis management   b. Workflow
    c. CIFMS   d. Performance measurement

12. In a human resources context, _____ or labor _____ is the rate at which an employer gains and loses employees. Simple ways to describe it are 'how long employees tend to stay' or 'the rate of traffic through the revolving door.' _____ is measured for individual companies and for their industry as a whole. If an employer is said to have a high _____ relative to its competitors, it means that employees of that company have a shorter average tenure than those of other companies in the same industry.

    a. Continuous   b. Turnover
    c. Ten year occupational employment projection   d. Career portfolios

13. _____ in engineering is a method of manufacturing in which the entire production process is controlled by computer. The traditional separated process methods are joined through a computer by CIM. This integration allows that the processes exchange information with each other and they are able to initiate actions.

    a. 28-hour day   b. 1990 Clean Air Act
    c. 33 Strategies of War   d. Computer-integrated manufacturing

14. In corporate finance, _____ or _____ is an estimate of true economic profit after making corrective adjustments to GAAP accounting, including deducting the opportunity cost of equity capital. _____ can be measured as Net Operating Profit After Taxes(or NOPAT) less the money cost of capital. _____ is similar in nature to that of calculating another financial performance measure - Residual Income , however, there are a few complexities involved with coming up with the elements for calculating _____ over RI such as the myriad adjustments that might be made to NOPAT before it is suitable for the formula below.

    a. A4e   b. Economic value added
    c. AAAI   d. A Stake in the Outcome

15. The _____ is an expected return that the provider of capital plans to earn on their investment.

Capital (money) used for funding a business should earn returns for the capital providers who risk their capital. For an investment to be worthwhile, the expected return on capital must be greater than the _____.

    a. Capital intensive   b. Cost of capital
    c. 1990 Clean Air Act   d. Weighted average cost of capital

Chapter 18. Organizational Design, Responsibility Accounting, and Evaluation

16. _____ refers to the difference between the cost of materials purchased by a company plus the cost of the labor to assemble a product and the price at which the company sells the product. An example is the price of gasoline at the pump over the price of the oil in it. In national accounts used in macroeconomics, it refers to the contribution of the factors of production, i.e., land, labor, and capital goods, to raising the value of a product and corresponds to the incomes received by the owners of these factors.

   a. Minimum wage   b. Rehn-Meidner Model
   c. Deregulation   d. Value added

17. The phrase mergers and _____s refers to the aspect of corporate strategy, corporate finance and management dealing with the buying, selling and combining of different companies that can aid, finance, or help a growing company in a given industry grow rapidly without having to create another business entity.

An _____, also known as a takeover or a buyout, is the buying of one company (the 'target') by another. An _____ may be friendly or hostile.

   a. Acquisition   b. A4e
   c. A Stake in the Outcome   d. AAAI

18. In finance, _____ are considered liabilities of the business that are to be settled in cash within the fiscal year or the operating cycle, whichever period is longer.

For example accounts payable for goods, services or supplies that were purchased for use in the operation of the business and payable within a normal period of time would be _____.

Bonds, mortgages and loans that are payable over a term exceeding one year would be fixed liabilities.

   a. Current liabilities   b. Generally accepted accounting principles
   c. Depreciation   d. Matching principle

19. In business and accounting, _____s are everything of value that is owned by a person or company. Any property or object of value that one possesses, usually considered as applicable to the payment of one's debts is considered an _____. Simplistically stated, _____s are things of value that can be readily converted into cash.

   a. A Stake in the Outcome   b. A4e
   c. AAAI   d. Asset

20. In economics, _____ is a decrease in the general price level of goods and services. _____ occurs when the annual inflation rate falls below zero percent, resulting in an increase in the real value of money -- a negative inflation rate. This should not be confused with disinflation, a slow-down in the inflation rate (i.e. when the inflation decreases, but still remains positive.)

   a. Productivity management   b. Human capital
   c. Deflation   d. Leading indicator

21. In economics, _____ is a rise in the general level of prices of goods and services in an economy over a period of time. When the general price level rises, each unit of the functional currency buys fewer goods and services; consequently, _____ is a decline in the real value of money--a loss of purchasing power in the internal medium of exchange which is also the monetary unit of account in an economy. A chief measure of general price-level _____ is the general _____ rate, which is the percentage change in a general price index (normally the Consumer Price Index) over time.
- a. A4e
- b. A Stake in the Outcome
- c. Economy
- d. Inflation

22. In economics and sociology, an _____ is any factor (financial or non-financial) that enables or motivates a particular course of action, or counts as a reason for preferring one choice to the alternatives. It is an expectation that encourages people to behave in a certain way. Since human beings are purposeful creatures, the study of _____ structures is central to the study of all economic activity (both in terms of individual decision-making and in terms of co-operation and competition within a larger institutional structure.)
- a. AAAI
- b. A4e
- c. A Stake in the Outcome
- d. Incentive

23. A chief executive officer (_____) or chief executive is one of the highest-ranking corporate officer (executive) or administrator in charge of total management. An individual selected as President and _____ of a corporation, company, organization, or agency, reports to the board of directors. In internal communication and press releases, many companies capitalize the term and those of other high positions, even when they are not proper nouns.
- a. Chief executive officer
- b. Portfolio manager
- c. Director of communications
- d. CEO

Chapter 19. Transfer Pricing

1. In economics and sociology, an _____ is any factor (financial or non-financial) that enables or motivates a particular course of action, or counts as a reason for preferring one choice to the alternatives. It is an expectation that encourages people to behave in a certain way. Since human beings are purposeful creatures, the study of _____ structures is central to the study of all economic activity (both in terms of individual decision-making and in terms of co-operation and competition within a larger institutional structure.)
   a. Incentive
   b. AAAI
   c. A4e
   d. A Stake in the Outcome

2. _____ refers to the pricing of contributions (assets, tangible and intangible, services, and funds) transferred within an organization. For example, goods from the production division may be sold to the marketing division, or goods from a parent company may be sold to a foreign subsidiary. Since the prices are set within an organization (i.e. controlled), the typical market mechanisms that establish prices for such transactions between third parties may not apply.
   a. Price floor
   b. Price ceiling
   c. Transfer pricing
   d. Pricing

3. _____ is one of the four Ps of the marketing mix. The other three aspects are product, promotion, and place. It is also a key variable in microeconomic price allocation theory.
   a. Penetration pricing
   b. Price floor
   c. Transfer pricing
   d. Pricing

4. In economics, business, retail, and accounting, a _____ is the value of money that has been used up to produce something, and hence is not available for use anymore. In economics, a _____ is an alternative that is given up as a result of a decision. In business, the _____ may be one of acquisition, in which case the amount of money expended to acquire it is counted as _____.
   a. Cost
   b. Fixed costs
   c. Cost overrun
   d. Cost allocation

5. _____ is a concept in economics which refers to the extent to which an enterprise or a nation actually uses its installed productive capacity. Thus, it refers to the relationship between actual output that 'is' produced with the installed equipment and the potential output which 'could' be produced with it, if capacity was fully used.

   If market demand grows, _____ will rise.

   a. Diseconomies of scale
   b. Multifactor productivity
   c. Factors of production
   d. Capacity utilization

6. _____ or economic opportunity loss is the value of the next best alternative forgone as the result of making a decision. _____ analysis is an important part of a company's decision-making processes but is not treated as an actual cost in any financial statement. The next best thing that a person can engage in is referred to as the _____ of doing the best thing and ignoring the next best thing to be done.
   a. AAAI
   b. Opportunity cost
   c. A4e
   d. A Stake in the Outcome

7. In economic theory, _____ is the competitive situation in any market where the conditions necessary for perfect competition are not satisfied. It is a market structure that does not meet the conditions of perfect competition.

Forms of _____ include:

- Monopoly, in which there is only one seller of a good.
- Oligopoly, in which there is a small number of sellers.
- Monopolistic competition, in which there are many sellers producing highly differentiated goods.
- Monopsony, in which there is only one buyer of a good.
- Oligopsony, in which there is a small number of buyers.

There may also be _____ in markets due to buyers or sellers lacking information about prices and the goods being traded.

There may also be _____ due to a time lag in a market.

a. AAAI
b. Imperfect competition
c. A4e
d. A Stake in the Outcome

8. In neoclassical economics and microeconomics, _____ describes the perfect being a market in which there are many small firms, all producing homogeneous goods. In the short term, such markets are productively inefficient as output will not occur where marginal cost is equal to average cost, but allocatively efficient, as output under _____ will always occur where marginal cost is equal to marginal revenue, and therefore where marginal cost equals average revenue. However, in the long term, such markets are both allocatively and productively efficient.

a. Perfect competition
b. Deflation
c. Market structure
d. Gross domestic product

9. _____ is an economic concept with commonplace familiarity. It is the price that a good or service is offered at, or will fetch, in the marketplace. It is of interest mainly in the study of microeconomics.

a. Market price
b. 28-hour day
c. 1990 Clean Air Act
d. 33 Strategies of War

10. _____ is a costing model that identifies activities in an organization and assigns the cost of each activity resource to all products and services according to the actual consumption by each: it assigns more indirect costs (overhead) into direct costs.

In this way an organization can establish the true cost of its individual products and services for the purposes of identifying and eliminating those which are unprofitable and lowering the prices of those which are overpriced.

In a business organization, the ABC methodology assigns an organization's resource costs through activities to the products and services provided to its customers.

a. A Stake in the Outcome
b. Indirect costs
c. A4e
d. Activity-based costing

Chapter 19. Transfer Pricing

11. _____ is the process of dispersing decision-making governance closer to the people or citizen. It includes the dispersal of administration or governance in sectors or areas like engineering, management science, political science, political economy, sociology and economics. _____ is also possible in the dispersal of population and employment.

   a. Business plan   b. Formula for Change
   c. Decentralization   d. Frenemy

12. In economics, a _____ is any economic system that effects its distribution of goods and services with prices and employing any form of money or debt tokens. Except for possible remote and primitive communities, all modern societies use _____s to allocate resources. However, _____s are not used for all resource allocation decisions today.

   a. 1990 Clean Air Act   b. 28-hour day
   c. 33 Strategies of War   d. Price system

13. The _____ is a private, not-for-profit organization whose primary purpose is to develop generally accepted accounting principles (GAAP) within the United States in the public's interest. The Securities and Exchange Commission (SEC) designated the _____ as the organization responsible for setting accounting standards for public companies in the U.S. It was created in 1973, replacing the Committee on Accounting Procedure (CAP) and the Accounting Principles Board (APB) of the American Institute of Certified Public Accountants (AICPA.)

The _____'s mission is 'to establish and improve standards of financial accounting and reporting for the guidance and education of the public, including issuers, auditors, and users of financial information.' To achieve this, _____ has five goals:

- Improve the usefulness of financial reporting by focusing on the primary characteristics of relevance and reliability, and on the qualities of comparability and consistency.
- Keep standards current to reflect changes in methods of doing business and in the economy.
- Consider promptly any significant areas of deficiency in financial reporting that might be improved through standard setting.
- Promote international convergence of accounting standards concurrent with improving the quality of financial reporting.
- Improve common understanding of the nature and purposes of information in financial reports.

The _____ is not a governmental body. The SEC has legal authority to establish financial accounting and reporting standards for publicly held companies under the Securities Exchange Act of 1934.

   a. Foreign direct investment   b. Prospero Business Suite
   c. Financial Accounting Standards Board   d. Chief risk officer

14. _____ is an advertisement in which a particular product specifically mentions a competitor by name for the express purpose of showing why the competitor is inferior to the product naming it.

This should not be confused with parody advertisements, where a fictional product is being advertised for the purpose of poking fun at the particular advertisement, nor should it be confused with the use of a coined brand name for the purpose of comparing the product without actually naming an actual competitor. ('Wikipedia tastes better and is less filling than the Encyclopedia Galactica.')

Chapter 19. Transfer Pricing

In the 1980s, during what has been referred to as the cola wars, soft-drink manufacturer Pepsi ran a series of advertisements where people, caught on hidden camera, in a blind taste test, chose Pepsi over rival Coca-Cola.

a. 33 Strategies of War
c. 28-hour day

b. 1990 Clean Air Act
d. Comparative advertising

Chapter 20. Strategy, Balanced Scorecards, and Incentive Systems

1. The _____ is a performance management tool for measuring whether the smaller-scale operational activities of a company are aligned with its larger-scale objectives in terms of vision and strategy.

By focusing not only on financial outcomes but also on the operational, marketing and developmental inputs to these, the _____ helps provide a more comprehensive view of a business, which in turn helps organizations act in their best long-term interests. This tool is also being used to address business response to climate change and greenhouse gas emissions.

   a. Management development
   b. Commercial management
   c. Balanced scorecard
   d. Middle management

2. In economics and sociology, an _____ is any factor (financial or non-financial) that enables or motivates a particular course of action, or counts as a reason for preferring one choice to the alternatives. It is an expectation that encourages people to behave in a certain way. Since human beings are purposeful creatures, the study of _____ structures is central to the study of all economic activity (both in terms of individual decision-making and in terms of co-operation and competition within a larger institutional structure.)
   a. A4e
   b. AAAI
   c. Incentive
   d. A Stake in the Outcome

3. In economics, _____s are key economic variables that economists used to predict a new phase of the business cycle. A _____ is one that changes before the economy does; a lagging indicator is one that changes after the economy has changed. Examples of _____s include stock prices, which often improve or worsen before a similar change in the economy.
   a. Human capital
   b. Perfect competition
   c. Deflation
   d. Leading indicator

4. _____ is the process whereby an organization establishes the parameters within which programs, investments, and acquisitions are reaching the desired results. Performance Reference Model of the Federal Enterprise Architecture, 2005.

This process of measuring performance often requires the use of statistical evidence to determine progress toward specific defined organizational objectives.

There are many types of measurements.

   a. CIFMS
   b. Workflow
   c. Crisis management
   d. Performance measurement

5. _____ is an area of knowledge within organizational theory that studies models and theories about the way an organization learns and adapts.

In Organizational development (OD), learning is a characteristic of an adaptive organization, i.e., an organization that is able to sense changes in signals from its environment (both internal and external) and adapt accordingly.

   a. AAAI
   b. A4e
   c. Organizational learning
   d. A Stake in the Outcome

6. _____ is subcontracting a process, such as product design or manufacturing, to a third-party company. The decision to outsource is often made in the interest of lowering cost or making better use of time and energy costs, redirecting or conserving energy directed at the competencies of a particular business, or to make more efficient use of land, labor, capital, (information) technology and resources. _____ became part of the business lexicon during the 1980s.

   a. Operant conditioning
   b. Opinion leadership
   c. Unemployment insurance
   d. Outsourcing

7. In a human resources context, _____ or labor _____ is the rate at which an employer gains and loses employees. Simple ways to describe it are 'how long employees tend to stay' or 'the rate of traffic through the revolving door.' _____ is measured for individual companies and for their industry as a whole. If an employer is said to have a high _____ relative to its competitors, it means that employees of that company have a shorter average tenure than those of other companies in the same industry.

   a. Career portfolios
   b. Ten year occupational employment projection
   c. Continuous
   d. Turnover

8. _____ is an advertisement in which a particular product specifically mentions a competitor by name for the express purpose of showing why the competitor is inferior to the product naming it.

This should not be confused with parody advertisements, where a fictional product is being advertised for the purpose of poking fun at the particular advertisement, nor should it be confused with the use of a coined brand name for the purpose of comparing the product without actually naming an actual competitor. ('Wikipedia tastes better and is less filling than the Encyclopedia Galactica.')

In the 1980s, during what has been referred to as the cola wars, soft-drink manufacturer Pepsi ran a series of advertisements where people, caught on hidden camera, in a blind taste test, chose Pepsi over rival Coca-Cola.

   a. 28-hour day
   b. 33 Strategies of War
   c. 1990 Clean Air Act
   d. Comparative advertising

9. In economics, business, retail, and accounting, a _____ is the value of money that has been used up to produce something, and hence is not available for use anymore. In economics, a _____ is an alternative that is given up as a result of a decision. In business, the _____ may be one of acquisition, in which case the amount of money expended to acquire it is counted as _____.

   a. Fixed costs
   b. Cost allocation
   c. Cost overrun
   d. Cost

10. In business and engineering, _____ is the term used to describe the complete process of bringing a new product or service to market. There are two parallel paths involved in the _____ process: one involves the idea generation, product design, and detail engineering; the other involves market research and marketing analysis. Companies typically see _____ as the first stage in generating and commercializing new products within the overall strategic process of product life cycle management used to maintain or grow their market share.

   a. 1990 Clean Air Act
   b. 28-hour day
   c. 33 Strategies of War
   d. New product development

Chapter 20. Strategy, Balanced Scorecards, and Incentive Systems

11. In organizational development (OD), _____ is a series of actions taken by a Process Owner to identify, analyze and improve existing processes within an organization to meet new goals and objectives. These actions often follow a specific methodology or strategy to create successful results. A sampling of these are listed below.
    a. Product innovation
    b. Process improvement
    c. Letter of resignation
    d. Supervisory board

12. In business and engineering, new _____ is the term used to describe the complete process of bringing a new product or service to market. There are two parallel paths involved in the NProduct development process: one involves the idea generation, product design, and detail engineering; the other involves market research and marketing analysis. Companies typically see new _____ as the first stage in generating and commercializing new products within the overall strategic process of product life cycle management used to maintain or grow their market share.
    a. Product development
    b. 33 Strategies of War
    c. 28-hour day
    d. 1990 Clean Air Act

13. _____ refers to metrics and measures of output from production processes, per unit of input. Labor _____, for example, is typically measured as a ratio of output per labor-hour, an input. _____ may be conceived of as a metrics of the technical or engineering efficiency of production.
    a. Value engineering
    b. Master production schedule
    c. Remanufacturing
    d. Productivity

14. The loyalty business model is a business model used in strategic management in which company resources are employed so as to increase the loyalty of customers and other stakeholders in the expectation that corporate objectives will be met or surpassed. A typical example of this type of model is: quality of product or service leads to customer satisfaction, which leads to _____, which leads to profitability.

Fredrick Reichheld (1996) expanded the loyalty business model beyond customers and employees.

    a. 28-hour day
    b. 33 Strategies of War
    c. 1990 Clean Air Act
    d. Customer loyalty

15. _____ is the activity that the selling organization undertakes to reduce customer account defections. The success of this activity is when the customer account places an additional order before a 12-month period has expired. Note that ideally these orders will need to contribute similar financial amounts to the previous 12 months.
    a. Business rule
    b. Foreign ownership
    c. Process automation
    d. Customer retention

16. _____, a business term, is a measure of how products and services supplied by a company meet or surpass customer expectation. It is seen as a key performance indicator within business and is part of the four perspectives of a Balanced Scorecard.

In a competitive marketplace where businesses compete for customers, _____ is seen as a key differentiator and increasingly has become a key element of business strategy.

    a. Foreign ownership
    b. Critical Success Factor
    c. Customer satisfaction
    d. Horizontal integration

Chapter 20. Strategy, Balanced Scorecards, and Incentive Systems

17. _____, in strategic management and marketing is, according to Carlton O'Neal, the percentage or proportion of the total available market or market segment that is being serviced by a company. It can be expressed as a company's sales revenue (from that market) divided by the total sales revenue available in that market. It can also be expressed as a company's unit sales volume (in a market) divided by the total volume of units sold in that market.

a. Green marketing
b. Marketing plan
c. Business-to-business
d. Market share

18. In decision theory and estimation theory, the _____ of an estimator, $\hat{\theta}$, of an unknown parameter of the distribution, θ, is the expected value of the loss function

$$R(\theta, \hat{\theta}) = \mathbb{E}_\theta L(\theta, \hat{\theta}) = \int L(\theta, \hat{\theta}) \, dP_\theta.$$

where dP_θ is a probability measure parametrized by θ.

- For a scalar parameter θ and a quadratic loss function,

$$L(\theta, \hat{\theta}) = (\theta - \hat{\theta})^2$$

the _____ function becomes the mean squared error of the estimate,

$$R(\theta, \hat{\theta}) = E_\theta(\theta - \hat{\theta})^2$$

- In density estimation, the unknown parameter is probability density itself. The loss function is typically chosen to be a norm in an appropriate function space. For example, for L^2 norm,

$$L(f, \hat{f}) = \|f - \hat{f}\|_2^2$$

the _____ function becomes the mean integrated squared error

$$R(f, \hat{f}) = E\|f - \hat{f}\|^2$$

a. Financial modeling
b. Linear model
c. Risk
d. Risk aversion

19. _____ is a business Advocate term for an element which is necessary for an organization or project to achieve its mission. They are the critical factors or activities required for ensuring the success of your business. The term was initially used in the world of data analysis, and business analysis.

a. Business hours
b. Collaborative leadership
c. Critical success factor
d. Customer satisfaction

Chapter 20. Strategy, Balanced Scorecards, and Incentive Systems

20. _____ is the difference between the revenues earned from and the costs associated with the customer relationship in a specified period.

According to Philip Kotler,'a profitable customer is a person, household or a company that overtime, yields a revenue stream that exceeds by an acceptable amount the company's cost stream of attracting, selling and servicing the customer'

Although _____ is nothing more than the result of applying the business concept of profit to a customer relationship, measuring the profitability of a firm's customers or customer groups can often deliver useful business insights.

Quite often a very small percentage of the firm's best customers will account for a large portion of firm profit.

    a. Factory overhead
    c. Profit center
    b. Customer profitability
    d. Process costing

21. The _____ percentage shows how profitable a company's assets are in generating revenue.

_____ can be computed as:

$$ROA = \frac{\text{Net Income} + \text{Interest Expense} - \text{Interest Tax savings}}{\text{Average Total Assets}}$$

This number tells you what the company can do with what it has, i.e. how many dollars of earnings they derive from each dollar of assets they control. Its a useful number for comparing competing companies in the same industry.

    a. P/E ratio
    c. Return on assets
    b. Return on equity
    d. Return on Capital Employed

22. In business and accounting, _____s are everything of value that is owned by a person or company. Any property or object of value that one possesses, usually considered as applicable to the payment of one's debts is considered an _____. Simplistically stated, _____s are things of value that can be readily converted into cash.
    a. A Stake in the Outcome
    c. AAAI
    b. Asset
    d. A4e

23. A chief executive officer (_____) or chief executive is one of the highest-ranking corporate officer (executive) or administrator in charge of total management. An individual selected as President and _____ of a corporation, company, organization, or agency, reports to the board of directors. In internal communication and press releases, many companies capitalize the term and those of other high positions, even when they are not proper nouns.
    a. Chief executive officer
    c. Director of communications
    b. Portfolio manager
    d. CEO

Chapter 20. Strategy, Balanced Scorecards, and Incentive Systems

24. The _____ of 2002 (Pub.L. 107-204, 116 Stat. 745, enacted July 30, 2002), also known as the Public Company Accounting Reform and Investor Protection Act of 2002 and commonly called Sarbanes-Oxley, Sarbox or SOX, is a United States federal law enacted on July 30, 2002, as a reaction to a number of major corporate and accounting scandals including those affecting Enron, Tyco International, Adelphia, Peregrine Systems and WorldCom.
    a. Fair Labor Standards Act
    b. Sarbanes-Oxley Act of 2002
    c. Letter of credit
    d. Sarbanes-Oxley Act

25. The _____, also known as the Public Company Accounting Reform and Investor Protection Act of 2002 and commonly called Sarbanes-Oxley, Sarbox or SOX, is a United States federal law enacted on July 30, 2002, as a reaction to a number of major corporate and accounting scandals including those affecting Enron, Tyco International, Adelphia, Peregrine Systems and WorldCom.
    a. Letter of credit
    b. Munn v. Illinois
    c. MacPherson v. Buick Motor Co.
    d. Sarbanes-Oxley Act of 2002

26. _____ are outcomes that are not (or not limited to) the results originally intended in a particular situation. The unintended results may be foreseen or unforeseen, but they should be the logical or likely results of the action. For example, historians have speculated that if the Treaty of Versailles had not imposed such harsh conditions on Germany, World War II would not have occurred.
    a. Unintended consequences
    b. A4e
    c. AAAI
    d. A Stake in the Outcome

27. _____ is the process of comparing the cost, cycle time, productivity, or quality of a specific process or method to another that is widely considered to be an industry standard or best practice. Essentially, _____ provides a snapshot of the performance of your business and helps you understand where you are in relation to a particular standard. The result is often a business case for making changes in order to make improvements.
    a. Complementors
    b. Benchmarking
    c. Cost leadership
    d. Competitive heterogeneity

28. _____ are a system of financial incentives designed to keep an employee from leaving the company. These can include employee stock options which will not vest for several years but are more often contractual obligations to give back lucrative bonuses or other compensation if the employee leaves for another company.

_____ are a response by the companies in industries where it is common for highly compensated employees to frequently move from one firm to another, often before the company feels that it has earned a return on the investment in the employee.

   a. Golden hello
   b. Cross-docking
   c. Process automation
   d. Golden handcuffs

29. A _____ is a form of periodic payment from an employer to an employee, which may be specified in an employment contract. It is contrasted with piece wages, where each job, hour or other unit is paid separately, rather than on a periodic basis.

From the point of a view of running a business, _____ can also be viewed as the cost of acquiring human resources for running operations, and is then termed personnel expense or _____ expense.

Chapter 20. Strategy, Balanced Scorecards, and Incentive Systems 113

a. Training and development
b. Human resources
c. Human resource management
d. Salary

30. In finance, an _____ is a contract between a buyer and a seller that gives the buyer the right--but not the obligation-- to buy or to sell a particular asset (the underlying asset) at a later day at an agreed price. In return for granting the _____, the seller collects a payment (the premium) from the buyer. A call _____ gives the buyer the right to buy the underlying asset; a put _____ gives the buyer of the _____ the right to sell the underlying asset.
   a. A4e
   b. A Stake in the Outcome
   c. Option
   d. AAAI

31. An _____ is a formal scheme used to promote or encourage specific actions or behavior by a specific group of people during a defined period of time. _____s are particularly used in business management to motivate employees, and in sales in order to attract and retain customers. The scientific literature also refers to this concept as Pay for Performance.
   a. A4e
   b. A Stake in the Outcome
   c. AAAI
   d. Incentive program

32. _____ is about the mental processes regarding choice, or choosing. It explains the processes that an individual undergoes to make choices. In organizational behavior study, _____ is a motivation theory first proposed by Victor Vroom of the Yale School of Management.
   a. AAAI
   b. A4e
   c. A Stake in the Outcome
   d. Expectancy theory

33. A _____ is a relatively new executive level position at a corporation, company, organization typically reporting directly to the CEO or board of directors. The _____ is responsible for a brand's image, experience, and promise, and propagating it throughout all aspects of the company. The brand officer oversees marketing, advertising, design, public relations and customer service departments.
   a. Director of communications
   b. Purchasing manager
   c. Chief brand officer
   d. Chief executive officer

34. In political science and economics, the _____ or agency dilemma treats the difficulties that arise under conditions of incomplete and asymmetric information when a principal hires an agent, such as the problem that the two may not have the same interests, while the principal is, presumably, hiring the agent to pursue the interests of the former.

Various mechanisms may be used to try to align the interests of the agent with those of the principal, such as piece rates/commissions, profit sharing, efficiency wages, performance measurement (including financial statements), the agent posting a bond, or fear of firing. The _____ is found in most employer/employee relationships, for example, when stockholders hire top executives of corporations.

   a. Principal-agent problem
   b. 33 Strategies of War
   c. 1990 Clean Air Act
   d. 28-hour day

35. _____ has become one of the most popular theories in organizational psychology.

Goal setting has been a formula used for acheivement since the early 1800s. The form and pattern has cahanged drastically over the years and there is still much debate as to what is the most efective pattern to follow.

a. Human relations
b. Job satisfaction
c. Corporate Culture
d. Goal-setting theory

36. An _____ is an economic concept that relates to the cost incurred by an entity (such as organizations) associated with problems such as divergent management-shareholder objectives and information asymmetry. The costs consist of two main sources:

1. The costs inherently associated with using an agent (e.g., the risk that agents will use organizational resource for their own benefit) and
2. The costs of techniques used to mitigate the problems associated with using an agent (e.g., the costs of producing financial statements or the use of stock options to align executive interests to shareholder interests.)

Though effects of _____ are present in any agency relationship, the term is most used in business contexts.

The information asymmetry that exists between shareholders and the Chief Executive Officer is generally considered to be a classic example of a principal-agent problem. The agent (the manager) is working on behalf of the principal (the shareholders), who does not observe the actions of the agent.

a. AAAI
b. A Stake in the Outcome
c. Agency cost
d. A4e

37. An _____ is a practitioner of accountancy, which is the measurement, disclosure or provision of assurance about financial information that helps managers, investors, tax authorities and other decision makers make resource allocation decisions.

The word '_____' is derived from the French 'Compter' which took its origin from the Latin 'Computare'. The word was formerly written in English as 'Accomptant', but in process of time the word, which was always pronounced by dropping the 'p', became gradually changed both in pronunciation and in orthography to its present form.

a. A Stake in the Outcome
b. AAAI
c. A4e
d. Accountant

38. _____ was a writer, management consultant, and self-described 'social ecologist.' Widely considered to be 'the father of modern management,' his 39 books and countless scholarly and popular articles explored how humans are organized across all sectors of society--in business, government and the nonprofit world. His writings have predicted many of the major developments of the late twentieth century, including privatization and decentralization; the rise of Japan to economic world power; the decisive importance of marketing; and the emergence of the information society with its necessity of lifelong learning. In 1959, Drucker coined the term 'knowledge worker' and later in his life considered knowledge work productivity to be the next frontier of management.

a. Jacques Al-Salawat Nasruddin Nasser
b. Chrissie Hynde
c. Peter Ferdinand Drucker
d. Debora L. Spar

39. _____ refers to the structured transmission of data between organizations by electronic means. It is used to transfer electronic documents from one computer system to another (ie) from one trading partner to another trading partner. It is more than mere E-mail; for instance, organizations might replace bills of lading and even checks with appropriate _____ messages.

   a. A Stake in the Outcome   b. AAAI
   c. Electronic data interchange   d. A4e

40. _____ is a company's financial statement that indicates how the revenue is transformed into the net income The purpose of the _____ is to show managers and investors whether the company made or lost money during the period being reported.

The important thing to remember about an _____ is that it represents a period of time.

   a. A4e   b. AAAI
   c. A Stake in the Outcome   d. Income statement

Chapter 1
1. d	2. d	3. d	4. d	5. a	6. d	7. c	8. b	9. a	10. b
11. b	12. b	13. d	14. b	15. d	16. d	17. d	18. a	19. b	20. d
21. d	22. c	23. a	24. a	25. d	26. d	27. d	28. d		

Chapter 2
1. d	2. d	3. d	4. d	5. a	6. d	7. d	8. d	9. d	10. d
11. b	12. b	13. a	14. d	15. d	16. b	17. d	18. d	19. d	20. c
21. b	22. d	23. d	24. c	25. b	26. b	27. a	28. d	29. c	30. a
31. b	32. c	33. d	34. b	35. a	36. a				

Chapter 3
1. c	2. b	3. d	4. d	5. d	6. b	7. d	8. d	9. c	10. d
11. c	12. c	13. d	14. d	15. d	16. c	17. d	18. d	19. b	20. b
21. d	22. c	23. b	24. d	25. d	26. b	27. d	28. d	29. b	30. c
31. b	32. d								

Chapter 4
| 1. d | 2. c | 3. d | 4. b | 5. a | 6. d | 7. d | 8. c | 9. d | 10. a |
| 11. d | 12. d | 13. d | 14. d | | | | | | |

Chapter 5
| 1. d | 2. a | 3. b | 4. d | 5. d | 6. b | 7. d | 8. b | 9. c | 10. a |
| 11. c | 12. d | 13. a | 14. c | 15. d | | | | | |

Chapter 6
1. b	2. d	3. c	4. a	5. d	6. a	7. d	8. b	9. d	10. b
11. b	12. d	13. b	14. a	15. d	16. d	17. a	18. d	19. d	20. d
21. b									

Chapter 7
1. c	2. b	3. a	4. a	5. b	6. d	7. d	8. d	9. a	10. b
11. a	12. b	13. b	14. d	15. d	16. d	17. a	18. d	19. b	20. c
21. d	22. d	23. b	24. b	25. d	26. a	27. b	28. d	29. d	30. d
31. d	32. b	33. d	34. c	35. c	36. b	37. d	38. d	39. d	40. d
41. d	42. a	43. b	44. c	45. b	46. d				

Chapter 8
| 1. d | 2. a | 3. d | 4. c | 5. a | 6. a | 7. c | 8. a | 9. b | 10. a |

Chapter 9
| 1. d | 2. d | 3. a | 4. d | 5. a | 6. a | 7. d | 8. d | 9. a | 10. a |
| 11. d | 12. b | 13. b | 14. a | | | | | | |

ANSWER KEY

Chapter 10
1. b 2. d 3. b 4. d 5. d 6. d 7. d 8. d 9. c 10. d
11. b 12. d 13. c 14. b 15. c

Chapter 11
1. d 2. d 3. b 4. d 5. d 6. d 7. d 8. b 9. d 10. d
11. c 12. d 13. d 14. c 15. c 16. d 17. d 18. d 19. d 20. d
21. d 22. d 23. b 24. a 25. d 26. c 27. d 28. c 29. d 30. c
31. d

Chapter 12
1. b 2. a 3. b 4. d 5. a 6. d 7. d 8. d 9. d 10. d
11. d 12. b 13. d 14. b 15. d 16. d 17. d 18. d 19. d 20. a

Chapter 13
1. b 2. c 3. b 4. a 5. d 6. b 7. c 8. a 9. d 10. d
11. a 12. d 13. c 14. b 15. d 16. d 17. d 18. a 19. d 20. d
21. c 22. a

Chapter 14
1. b 2. d 3. a 4. d 5. c 6. a 7. b 8. d 9. d 10. d
11. d 12. d 13. d 14. d 15. d 16. c 17. a 18. d 19. b 20. d
21. d 22. c 23. a 24. a 25. a 26. c 27. d 28. d 29. d 30. a
31. a 32. b 33. a 34. d 35. b

Chapter 15
1. a 2. d 3. d 4. d 5. d 6. a 7. d 8. a 9. a 10. d
11. d 12. d 13. b 14. d 15. c 16. a 17. d 18. d 19. d 20. c
21. d 22. d 23. d 24. d 25. a 26. c 27. c 28. c 29. d 30. d
31. d 32. b 33. a 34. b

Chapter 16
1. c 2. d 3. c 4. d 5. a 6. a 7. b 8. c 9. c 10. d
11. d 12. d 13. d 14. b 15. c 16. d 17. b 18. d 19. b 20. d
21. d 22. d 23. a 24. d 25. d 26. d 27. b

Chapter 17
1. c 2. d 3. d 4. d 5. c 6. d 7. b 8. d 9. b 10. d
11. a 12. d 13. d 14. b 15. b 16. b 17. d

Chapter 18
1. c 2. b 3. d 4. d 5. c 6. d 7. d 8. c 9. d 10. d
11. d 12. b 13. d 14. b 15. b 16. d 17. a 18. a 19. d 20. c
21. d 22. d 23. d

Chapter 19

| 1. a | 2. c | 3. d | 4. a | 5. d | 6. b | 7. b | 8. a | 9. a | 10. d |
| 11. c | 12. d | 13. c | 14. d | | | | | | |

Chapter 20

1. c	2. c	3. d	4. d	5. c	6. d	7. d	8. d	9. d	10. d
11. b	12. a	13. d	14. d	15. d	16. c	17. d	18. c	19. c	20. b
21. c	22. b	23. d	24. d	25. d	26. a	27. b	28. d	29. d	30. c
31. d	32. d	33. c	34. a	35. d	36. c	37. d	38. c	39. c	40. d

www.ingramcontent.com/pod-product-compliance
Lightning Source LLC
Chambersburg PA
CBHW082049230426
43670CB00016B/2830